JUDGING EXHIBITIONS
A Framework for Assessing Excellence

To Jim and Leo

JUDGING EXHIBITIONS
A Framework for Assessing Excellence

Beverly Serrell

Left Coast
Press Inc.

Walnut Creek, California

LEFT COAST PRESS, INC.
1630 North Main Street, #400
Walnut Creek, CA 94596
http://www.LCoastPress.com

**Left Coast
Press** Inc.

ISBN 1-59874-031-8 hardcover with compact disk

ISBN 1-59874-032-6 paperback with compact disk

Library of Congress Control Number: 2006921423

Printed in the United States of America

∞™ The paper used in this publication meets the minimum
requirements of American National Standard for Information
Sciences–Permanence of Paper for Printed Library Materials,
ANSI/NISO Z39.48–1992.

Book, cover, and CD design and production by Hannah Jennings Design.

06 07 08 09 10   5 4 3 2 1

The Excellent Judges project was supported in part by the
National Science Foundation under Grant No. 0118011. Any
opinions, findings, and conclusions or recommendations
expressed in this material are those of the author and do not
necessarily reflect the views of the National Science Foundation.

Table of Contents

Foreword

Judging Exhibitions: A Framework for Assessing Excellence not only shares the important results but also tells the lively story of an intriguing project: a collaborative inquiry into the mysteries of judgment. This is a brave thing to do, even when it is done by people who are highly practiced in making judgments–in this case, about the excellence of museum exhibitions. No matter how experienced, knowledgeable, and respected the judge, her/his judgment is never unquestionable.

Judgment always matters. It has to do with choice, commitment, value, and action. Judgment is also always indeterminate and mysterious. How is it possible, after all, to apply general standards of excellence, of truth, of goodness, of justice to unique individuals, artworks, exhibits, or actions? Yet we do it. We must do it: how else to use principles in the real world of particulars? But no generalization fits any singular reality perfectly. There is no formula; while we may get it right, we cannot prove it. Judgment must persuade; it cannot coerce.

I am always concerned about what I see as a common, stubborn desire to avoid judgment through standardization–for example, of that which is to be judged, on the one hand, and, on the other, of criteria to be used. Beverly Serrell and her collaborators have wisely balanced the desire to offer people guidelines that do some of the basic work of judgment with the realization that judgment remains an art of free minds that are open to the voices of other people, and to the uniqueness of each subject, material, and situation.

Many of us, as practitioners in differing fields but also as lovers of the aspirational values of democracy, have something to learn from this thoughtful, respectful, and eminently practical story of the creation of a framework to guide judgment.

Elizabeth Minnich

PhD Senior Fellow,
Association of American
Colleges and Universities

PART I

INTRODUCTION

Accountability is a challenging issue for institutions that offer educational exhibitions. Assessing, judging, evaluating, critiquing, and reviewing: Each of these activities requires a different set of definitions, c:riteria, and methods for measuring the exhibition's accomplishments, success, excellence, effectiveness–or missed opportunities. Each situation also varies in the number of people involved in the process, the duration of the activity, and the fate or usefulness of the product (e.g., the report, article, discussion, or award). Too often, the processes do not provide enough input from enough people or allow enough time for reflection, leading to ephemeral rather than long-lasting results. All types of assessments are useful; many are underused; and a few have unqualified benefits for the users. Doing something–anything–is better than doing nothing. This book presents the methods, reasons, and benefits of doing one type of assessment that can have widespread positive effects on individuals who work for museums and the people who visit them.

How and Why
the Framework Got Developed

Since the 1970s I've worked as an exhibition evaluator, served as a judge for the American Association of Museums (AAM) exhibition awards, reviewed exhibitions for museum journals, and spoken as a panel member for the exhibition critique session at AAM's annual conference. Living in Chicago, with a sizable pool of museum practitioners close by, I wanted to create an opportunity for a group of peers to meet repeatedly over a long period of time to review and critique exhibitions and then to develop a shared set of standards for making excellent museum exhibitions. I thought that if we could have enough time to think together, we could come up with a truly new and interesting way to judge excellence through a process or product that could have a lasting and positive impact on ourselves and on our work.

In July 2000, I sent a letter to the 100-plus members of the Chicago Museum Exhibitors Group (CMEG) outlining some of the issues with the current methods of judging excellence and inviting them to volunteer to become part of an ongoing discussion. There was no client, no schedule, and no money to do this. Still, I thought it would be fun: Would anyone else like to participate?

Twenty-one people responded to the invitation, and 13 showed up for the first meeting. Over the next four months we had seven two-hour evening meetings.

The Framework for Assessing Exhibitions from a Visitor-Centered Perspective did not emerge fully-formed

The Research Question

If different museum professionals used the same set of standards to review the same group of exhibitions, would their reviews agree on the degree of excellence for each of the exhibitions? And if not, why?

from our heads. When we first sat down together in July 2000, I acted as the facilitator and attempted to direct the discussion. We didn't know exactly where we were going with the topic of judging excellence or what to call ourselves. At times our discussions veered off in many directions. At one point, I asked everyone to use three different sets of criteria to judge one exhibition and report back on which one worked best. Instead they came back with five more tools! It was like herding cats.

The process was very open-ended. We discussed the issues in a rambling, free-flowing way. There was no schedule and no deadline. We had our research question (see sidebar on page 3), but we did not know what the answer would be or how we would answer it. The agenda evolved as we went along.

From August to November 2000, we visited eight exhibitions located in or near Chicago. They had diverse subjects, sizes, topics, and presentation techniques. Seven of the eight we chose were permanent exhibitions so we could easily revisit them. If we were to publish our comments about an exhibition, we wanted other people to be able to see the exhibition themselves and compare their reactions to ours.

Eight exhibitions in five different museums were visited by Chicago judges from July to November 2000

Jade at Field Museum
What Is An Animal? at Field Museum
The Endurance at Field Museum
Otters and Oil Don't Mix at Shedd Aquarium
Amazon Rising at Shedd Aquarium
A House Divided at Chicago Historical Society
Petroleum Planet at Museum of Science and Industry
Children's Garden at Garfield Park Conservatory

What We Built On

Our earliest versions of exhibition standards focused on presentation issues such as design, content, and accessibility, but they did not seem to substantially improve on the existing AAM Standards for Museum Exhibitions. After struggling with different versions of AAM criteria that were primarily related to what the museum had presented in the exhibition, we took a different tack. By the end of September 2000, we had narrowed our focus to criteria that related only to the visitor's experience. We began arguing about how to use the criteria rather than what the criteria should be. By eliminating judgments about the quality of the design and the accuracy or importance of the content, and by not attempting to judge intent, we made our task manageable and leveled the playing field: We were all visitors. We would judge exhibitions by how it felt to be in them, not what they said about themselves in a review or in a binder of PR materials, or showed in colorful slides.

Rather than try to make AAM's Standards "better," or replace them, we came up with something that was very different (and missing from AAM's criteria)–more focus on the visitor experience. We decided to focus exclusively on visitor-centered issues: what visitors could experience, where we could see evidence for visitors' needs and expectations, how the exhibitions might impact them. Our criteria reflected on and

I ended up just going back and rereading the AAM Standards, and I must say that I have greatly increased respect for them after struggling with the issues myself and hearing and reading everyone's comments.

Hannah Jennings

asked, What did the exhibition afford visitors for informal, educationally engaging exhibit experiences?

At the end of November 2000, the group had a prototype tool with fairly well-developed criteria and a protocol for using it. An article about it was published for the museum practitioner community in the National Association for Museum Exhibition *Exhibitionist* magazine (Serrell 2001), and I presented it as a workshop at the 2001 Visitor Studies Association conference.

Funding from NSF Helped

Feedback and wider scrutiny by our colleagues reinforced my idea to request a grant from the National Science Foundation (NSF) to support further development of the tool and its integration with broader educational theory and practice. We needed funding to move the tool to the next phase—doing more research on the questions of validity and reliability, getting help from an advisory board, and achieving the goal of broader acceptance, distribution, and use of the tool.

From April 2002 to September 2003, our project was supported by an NSF Small Grant for Exploratory Research. The grant allowed us to meet regularly in a central location in Chicago, pay for participants' parking, give them a stipend for their time, help support my part as project director, fund the development and maintenance of a new Web site, and contribute toward publication of the final results.

During the 18 months of NSF-funded research (plus a six-month nonfunded extension), we reviewed, revised, tested, and clarified the Criteria and Aspects of a framework and the layout of a handout. There were, in total, about a dozen iterations of the text and the design.

The most important difference between what we started out to do and what we completed was a shift in focus from measuring and comparing ratings of

There still seems to be a lot of overlap between the categories, though I'm not sure how to make them distinct without thinking about it further. Also, I like the idea of using the Criteria as points of discussion rather than as a means of calculating a score.

Workshop
participant,
July 2001

NSF Grant Request Summary

Serrell & Associates requests an 18-month Small Grant for Exploratory Research (SGER) totaling $95,500 to conduct research that seeks a valid and reliable way for museum professionals to judge the excellence of science exhibitions in museums from a visitor-experience point of view. This is a novel and untested idea for practitioners of exhibition development in science museums. The need for this research arises from a lack of agreed-upon standards of excellence (or even competence) for science museum exhibitions. Museums that receive funding from the National Science Foundation are called upon to document the effectiveness and merit of their exhibit projects, yet they have few shared, standardized methods to help them do so. An SGER would enable Serrell & Associates to conduct a series of meetings and seminars with local (Chicago) museum professionals and a national advisory panel to facilitate the development and testing of an audience-based, peer-reviewed criteria for recognizing excellence through empirical definitions and exemplars.

The research question for this project is: If different museum professionals used the same set of standards to visit, review, and judge the same group of exhibitions, would their ratings agree on the degree of excellence for each of the exhibitions? The proposed research methods will be informed by the science education research of John R. Frederiksen (University of California at Berkeley and the Educational Testing Service), who has developed techniques and criteria for performance evaluation of science teaching. His scoring methods incorporate direct and positive ways in which assessment can be used to improve science teaching. There are very clear parallels between Frederiksen's assessment techniques, which "make teachers aware of the characteristics of outstanding teaching that are shared values within the profession," and the goals of this project for science museum exhibit developers. The long-term goal of this research is to improve the quality of visitors' experiences in and satisfaction with science museum exhibitions.

exhibitions to making what we came to call "the Framework," with the primary function of professional development–a tool that could help people think more deeply about their work.

The names of all the judges and advisors who were involved are listed in the back of this book.

Over the last three years, I've heard from people throughout the United States and beyond–from individuals, to staff members within one institution, to casual professional groups similar to the Chicago Museum Exhibitors Group who started it all–who

At the first advisors meeting, in June 2002, we discussed the goals for the project and agreed that one outcome might be, that after using these Criteria, "Maybe next time you'd argue more strongly for some things that you knew were important."

have used the Framework. I am thrilled by the extent of its impact alongside other current efforts to define and promote best practices in museum exhibitions. People have used the Framework according to the format and protocol published in the handout; some have used it in museum studies classes. Some have taken the Framework's Criteria and modified them for their own uses. Don Hughes used it on a Monterey Bay Aquarium staff trip to review aquariums in Japan; evaluators Lynda Kelly at The Australian Museum, in Sydney, and Karen Graham at the Canadian Museum of Civilization, in Ottawa, have combined the Framework with other critique tools. These alternate uses are fine, because what we produced was not meant to be the last word or only way to apply the Framework. On the other hand, I also have heard that some people are using the Framework as a substitute for summative evaluation, and that's not so fine because it is not the same thing at all. (See the chart comparing different types of reviews on pages 92 and 93.)

The process of developing the Framework remains one of the most enjoyable professional experiences I've ever had. We gave ourselves the time to think critically about what we were doing, it took place in a very nonthreatening environment, and when the grant period was over, the Chicago group wanted to keep meeting for the social and mental stimulation of our wide-ranging discussions of museum exhibitions.

The funding was an important factor in sustaining the diligence and coherence of the group, as well as my perseverance. After we'd worked free for the first four months, the NSF grant sustained us, thankfully, for another 24.

We love it! What we have done is implement a series of regular exhibition critiques with a mix of museum staff and external people looking at exhibitions here and elsewhere.

Lynda Kelly

At first I have to admit I really chafed at working within these Criteria. I felt at the outset a little constrained. But then, going through the exercises, I felt it was really making me pay attention to some things that, if I was doing it in a more casual or less systematic way, I definitely would have blanked on.

Dan Spock

Eight exhibitions were visited by Chicago judges from April 2002 to September 2003

Underground Adventure at Field Museum
Messages from the Wilderness at Field Museum
The Milky Way Galaxy at Adler Planetarium
Genetics: Decoding Life at Museum of Science and Industry
The Swamp at Brookfield Zoo
Inventing Lab at Chicago Children's Museum
Play It Safe at Chicago Children's Museum
Wild Reef at Shedd Aquarium

The "Excellent Judges" Name

Hannah Jennings contributed to this section.

As is so often the case with grassroots groups, we started in a burst of enthusiasm, indignation, and hubris. We were going to whip out criteria that would reform how awards were awarded: a research-based, mathematical construct that would allow judges in different cities to rate different exhibitions fairly and to a common standard. Our hubris was tempered only by a sense of humor. At first it was a joke: If we were going to judge excellence in exhibitions, we should call ourselves the Excellent Judges. Unfortunately, no one came up with a real name that we could agree on, so we actually made Excellent Judges our working title– EJ for short.

We rapidly settled down and realized, with humility, that our product would not reach our original, unrealistic goals. As our thinking evolved, our emphasis shifted away from scoring systems and toward professional development and developing a shared vocabulary for the field. We went from judging exhibitions to judging ourselves. Of course, we always fall short of being excellent, but it's a goal to keep striving towards.

The Excellent Judges is an open club. Anyone who uses the Framework becomes one.

The Excellent Judges are you.

I thought that was a really hokey term at first. And then, you know, I'm kind of liking it, because now I'm an Excellent Judge, although I'm really not. But it has a unique psychological effect to it, I think, intended or not.

Excellent Judges workshop participant, 2002

I'm confused by your term "Excellent Judges" for the name of the project. To me, that means that these judges are excellent, which is not your meaning, I'm sure. I'd propose something like: Excellence Judges, Judges in Excellence, Judging Excellence, or Judging Exhibit Excellence.

Josh Gutwill

I think the name "Excellent Judges" has limited relevance: While it has been a recognizable working name for your team, it does not clearly describe your averred goals of professional development and visitor-centeredness. To my mind, "excellent" conveys arrogance rather than an examination of excellence, and "judges" suggests the act of critiquing rather than opening dialogue.

Lisa Hubbell

Anyone can be an Excellent Judge.

Although I was an early advocate of changing the name, my sense is that the better name just won out, while also contributing a twist of controversy that helped us refine the whole project. I like that organic element of this process.

Barbara Becker

11

What's in This Book and on the CD

The chapters in this book will review and describe what the Framework is, how to use it (and how not to use it), what the theoretical underpinnings are, and how it fits into the current and future assessments of exhibitions from a visitor-centered perspective.

Throughout the book there are frequently asked questions (FAQs), and many of the chapters are based on/in response to an FAQ.

The CD contains a 6-minute video of the Excellent Judges process–the orientation meeting, the exhibition visit, and the discussion meeting. The black-and-white photographs in the text show examples of exhibit elements that were reviewed during our project. The photographs on the CD are in color and have captions that are based on comments–reactions and feelings–made by a judge as he or she visited the exhibition and wrote notes. On the CD, you can link these comments to related information listed in the Framework.

Quotations throughout the book are unpublished remarks from personal communications with individuals who were involved in the project over the years as judges or advisors, in discussions following conference presentations (AAM '02 and '03, ASTC '03), or via e-mail.

Contributors to This Book

Many people helped develop the Framework and write this book. Biographical sketches of chapter contributors are at the end of the book. Here, special thanks go to these people: Mitch Allen, Sue Allen, Lorraine Bailey, Barbara Becker, Tamara Biggs, Joy Bivens, Colleen Blair, Barbara Ceiga, Patrice Ceisel, Barbara Clark, Kitty Connolly, Ben Dickow, Eugene Dillenburg, Doreen Finkelstein, Darcie Fohrman, Karen Furnweger, Marni Gittleman, Dianne Hanau-Strain, Donald Hughes, Hannah Jennings, Lynn LaBate, Nancy Levner, Frank Madsen, Ann Marshall, Viviane Meerbergen, Josie Menkin, Abner Mikva, Therese Quinn, Peter Serrell, Matt Sikora, Dan Spock, Mary Beth Trautwein, Charlie Walter, Stephanie Weaver, Kimberly Williams, Mara Williams, and The Cliff Dwellers Club.

We created a "mockumentory" video of the Framework process for this book in November 2005.

PART II

WHAT IS THE FRAMEWORK?

The Excellent Judges Framework is an enterprise that encompasses both a written list of Criteria and the actions associated with using that list. We call it an enterprise because the Framework poses stimulating challenges to first-time users. There are new terms to learn; it's a different way of thinking. To undertake the process of understanding the Framework and applying the Criteria requires energy and time. But the benefits are worth the effort.

The Purpose and the Process

The purpose of the Framework is to identify important characteristics of educational museum exhibitions and to assess the degree to which those traits are present in a given exhibition in a way that encourages an increase in those characteristics in future exhibitions.

The Framework is a process primarily of discussions among fellow museum colleagues and observations of an exhibition. Four Criteria frame both the discussions and the critical examination of the exhibition. The four Criteria are: Comfortable, Engaging, Reinforcing, and Meaningful. Each of these four Criteria has supporting, defining Aspects.

What Are "Criteria" and What Are "Aspects"?

Criteria are the standards by which exhibitions are to be assessed. These Criteria are essential and must be present in an exhibition if visitors are to be afforded excellent learning opportunities. Aspects are the building blocks of the Criteria. They are defining qualities that form a Criterion. They are designed to provide concrete examples of the things covered by each Criterion. There are four to eight Aspects for every Criterion. No single exhibit is expected to meet all the Aspects of a Criterion.

All the Criteria and their Aspects are related to creating comfortable, engaging, reinforcing, and meaningful educational experiences for visitors.

While the Excellent Judges Framework is ultimately a process, its tangible manifestation is a six-page document that's meant to be copied, written on, and discussed. The Framework form itself is printed in Part III of this book (pages 41 to 46). It contains the directions for use, a guide through a carefully structured process, and lists of the Criteria and their Aspects. There are spaces to take notes, assess the Aspects, and write ratings and Rationales.

What Are "Ratings" and What Are "Rationales"?

Ratings are the numbers and rubrics given by judges for each Criterion. There are six levels: 1 = Excellent, 2 = Very Good, 3 = Good, 4 = Acceptable, 5 = Misses opportunities, and 6 = Counterproductive. Ratings are based on the presence or absence of evidence of the Framework's Aspects seen by the assessor in the exhibition. (This will all make much more sense when you actually use the Framework! Watch the 6-minute video on the CD for an overview.)

Rationales are a judge's reasons for giving a particular rating level to a Criterion. Rationales should use the language of the Aspects to ensure that the scores are internally consistent and to create a growing set of evidence and a shared vocabulary for the group. Rationales and ratings are informed by Call-outs.

What Are "Call-Outs"?

During the process of using the Framework in an exhibition, judges write notes on the form, called "Call-outs." Call-outs are written during and at the end of an exhibition visit. They describe the scorer's feelings about both details and overall impressions while in the exhibition. These are used as evidence for creating a scorer's overall assessment. They are primarily for the scorer's own use but may be shared later in discussions about the exhibition.

A Process, Not a Checklist

The Excellent Judges (EJ) Framework addresses the difficulty of determining what makes an excellent exhibition by using an approach that both provides a yardstick and allows for the flexibility needed to honor the complexity inherent in exhibits. It describes and assesses the nature of the experiences that are known, through more than 50 years of established research, to most likely lead to free-choice learning. In other words, in an informal learning environment like a museum, these Aspects are likely to motivate visitors to choose to pay attention, spend time, become engaged, and be changed by the experience. This is what museum "learning" is all about.

At the same time, the Excellent Judges Framework builds upon years of collective experience in developing exhibitions from practitioners in the field. The Framework is not a to-do list of best practices and pointers, however. Such a document would not be able to address the intricacy and variety of exhibits or their development.

The EJ Framework takes the position that the excellence of an exhibit should be judged based on the potential of an exhibition to afford high-quality visitor experiences. Furthermore, the Framework assesses the important aspects of educational exhibitions from a visitor-centered perspective. The Framework is about defining the affordances–opportunities that enable excellent visitor learning experiences–that should be present in an exhibition.

The Framework is to be used by museum professionals. By participating in its process, professionals are given a common vocabulary, based in the Framework's Criteria, with which to describe excellence in

Although the Framework is aimed at professionals, it also puts you squarely in the place of the visitor. It helps me to think clearly about what aspects of a show I like and dislike and why. It makes concrete the principles we all know: make it relevant; make it accessible; put in plenty of seating. Doing the critique, especially in such a formal and repeatable way, brings these issues to prominence for me. I am coming to really understand how these principles are embodied in an exhibition and the consequences when they are not.

Kitty Connolly

those experiences and others. The process allows practitioners to become intimately familiar with a language of exhibition excellence–a language refined over several years–and integrate this vocabulary and the concepts it represents into their work.

The structure of the Framework, its process and, especially, its Criteria prompt practitioners to respond to an exhibit from a visitor-centered perspective and then report their experiences back to a group through discussion. Because the group consists of museum professionals, the members can articulate their experiences in terms that reflect their own expertise and that their colleagues can understand. The Framework allows professionals to use their own personal responses as visitors to refine and define broader principles concerning their work as museum practitioners.

The discussion-based nature of the Framework also can help a group of practitioners become better aware of each other. By participating in the Framework's process, shared ideas about exhibit development, museums, or other concepts important to the field will coalesce. At the very least, the discussions will make colleagues conscious of each other's views.

We sought to define Criteria of excellence in a way that would enable conversation among professionals and result in a better product for visitors. "It is, after all, the learning environment that is under the control of the museum" (Leinhardt and Knutson 2004). How can we make the most of it?

The Joy of Thinking

The outcome of using the Framework and participating in the discussions is not a grade of merit given to an exhibition or a punch list of items that need fixing, but rather the sheer enjoyment of thinking, reflecting, and learning. We engaged in thought processes and critical thinking exercises that most museum practitioners do not or cannot take the time to explore and enjoy. Our discussions had a "freedom of mind" in which we appreciated the value of being

- open-minded
- reflective
- challenging, but more likely to question than assert
- inclined to listen to many sides
- capable of making distinctions that hold difference in play rather than dividing in order to exclude
- desirous of persuading others rather than reducing them to silence by refuting them.

The Framework is a structure for thinking more openly, for listening more openly. The list above is based on Elizabeth Minnich's article on "Teaching Thinking" (Minnich 2003). Her remarks, although aimed at academics, are right on for us: "Will we differ? Yes, but if we talk together about what we are doing, sharing our questions, examples, and stories, we can develop a communal sense of what we are doing that will help us as we make our judgments."

I've used the Framework a number of times, both as a facilitator and as a participant, with staff members from various museums. I have used it to examine all types of exhibitions—science, natural history, art, history. Although I believe the Framework was first developed primarily for science exhibitions, it seems to transcend disciplines and works equally well with all. It also seems to work well with varying exhibition formats, whether object-based, hands-on, or a combination.

Gretchen Jennings

FAQ: How can one set of Criteria apply to very different exhibits?

Each of the four Criteria (Comfortable, Engaging, Reinforcing, and Meaningful) has applicability for a wide range of exhibit subjects, techniques, and bud-gets. We tested the Framework in 16 exhibitions in Chicago, and it's been used in that many again in other cities in the United States and abroad.

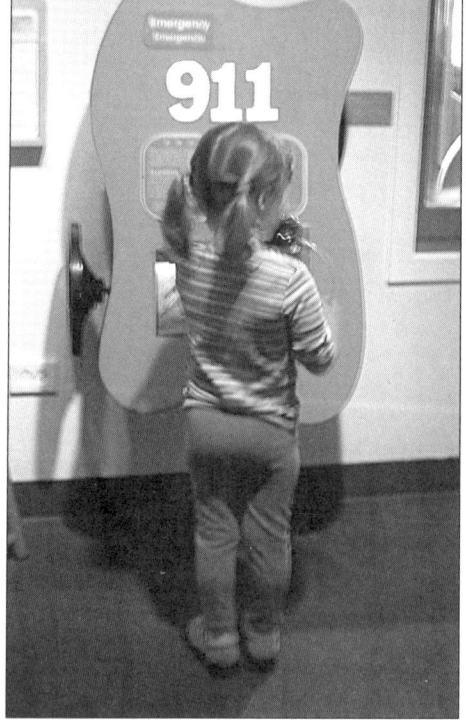

The two types of museums that have raised questions about the applicability of the Criteria are children's museums where the target audience is very young (under 5), and art museum exhibits where little or no interpretation is present. The latter will be discussed in the chapter on pages 84 to 87. In children's museums, the Framework works if the target audience includes adults and the exhibition directs interpretation at them as facilitators for an educational experience.

Some topics in children's museums are clearly meant for an audience that includes adults as mediators for kids' learning.

The Criterion of Comfortable is the one people question most often: What if the exhibition has a difficult or controversial topic that makes people feel uncomfortable? A person can have a sense of discomfort with a difficult exhibition topic if she understands the nature of the issues and the museum's intentions in presenting them. If it's clear to the visitor why this is so, the Comfortable Criterion may be assessed as positive.

By comfortable, we do not mean a warm and fuzzy feeling. "Comfortable" is a clear, cognitive understanding of what is going on and why–whether the topic is pleasant or horrifying. A lack of comfort can also be an intentional momentary or temporary one in the exhibition's design to create a sense of conflict that gets resolved in the overall experience.

Probably the most important Aspect of comfort that needs to be addressed in an exhibition with an uncomfortable topic is the one of authorship: The museum must make clear the biases and perspectives of the exhibit developers who are presenting the topic by answering these questions: What is fact or fiction, what is real or unreal? Who are the authors and what is their authority to speak on the topic?

FAQ: Can we really judge excellence?

Excellent museum exhibitions are elusive, both because they are rare, and because determining their excellence is difficult. Unlike the business world, where the standard measuring stick of "profitability" exists, the gauge of exhibition excellence has been, for the most part, subjective and vague, or at least not agreed upon. Furthermore, the complexity of an exhibition and lack of a precise quantitative measurement raises the question, Who judges? Do you hire outside experts or does the museum field create a cabal of peer reviewers, whose tastes might counter or compete with in-house stakeholders?

The problem with assessing excellence in museum exhibitions is that everyone has a different definition of excellence. Curators want the latest, most accurate

Comfort includes a section about authorship and biases and another about welcoming people from different groups and classes. But I'm not satisfied with these: I think "comfort" is too weak a label to encompass everything from racism and bias to exclusion of disabled people; and I still think that knowing who paid for an exhibit changes how I make sense of its messages.

Therese Quinn

content. Designers want a beautiful space. Marketing wants bodies through the door. These are all perfectly desirable characteristics or functions, and all are extremely important. We are not aiming to supplant or replace any of these viewpoints but to augment them with a deeper understanding of the experience itself. Indeed, we have to be able to take a visitor-centered perspective because we are in the business of creating visitor experiences. If we can't look at exhibits in terms of what features are likely to work for the audience, then we are simply wasting time and money–ours and the public's.

FAQ: Can we even define excellence after all?

Only imperfectly–not excellently! But this Framework gives museum practitioners a common starting point in discussions about excellence and takes the field forward in doing so. Excellence in exhibitions is a goal. We strive for it, and the process of striving is ongoing.

Taking a "Visitor-Centered Perspective"

The Criteria and Aspects of the Excellent Judges Framework are all visitor-centered in that they focus on and define exhibit functions that promote positive learning experiences for visitors in informal learning situations. The process of using the Framework by the judges is also visitor-centered.

Eugene Dillenburg and Ben Dickow contributed to this chapter.

To judge an exhibition's excellence from a visitor-centered perspective, the Framework's process does not ask participating museum professionals to try to guess what a visitor might think, but instead requires museum professionals to be themselves—as visitors to a museum exhibition. Visiting exhibits is integral to "doing" the Framework. In fact, first-time users of the EJ Framework are encouraged to assess an exhibition other than one they have worked on so they can distance themselves from any professional intents they may have had in developing the exhibition, such as content-specific learning goals.

The Excellent Judges have used holistic performance assessment to define and operationalize a framework that tackles the biggest possible questions of what we value. I think this team has done an outstanding job of selecting and refining the key Criteria and attributes that define that framework.

Sue Allen

The people in the gallery seemed to find the experience extremely approachable. Maybe it's not fair to cross my own experience into observations of other people there, but it just didn't feel like an especially daunting kind of an experience the way some museum experiences can be.

Dan Spock

Judges pay attention to the ambiance and emotive Aspects. This shiny, clean space was called the "Mud Room" —a lack of congruence between words and feelings noted by the EJs and visitors alike.

Although professionals have the insider perspective, the Framework's Criteria and process allow museum practitioners to break out of the "curse" of looking at exhibits only from the perspective of a professional, which may include looking at details of presentation (colors, design elegance, etc.), clever solutions to common building problems, or whether the exhibit meets the developer's content goals and objectives. Some of these things may impact a visitor's experience, but they are likely not to be on the minds of most visitors.

So how can we, as insiders, assume the proper perspective–to see things as visitors? Do we put ourselves in the visitors' shoes? Try to read their minds? Imagine what a "typical" visitor would think, feel, and do?

Nope. The tool asks you to be you: A person who enjoys museums, finds them interesting, thinks they are worthwhile. A person who, like most people, wants to be comfortable, wants to feel respected, wants to feel the time is well-spent. A person with a unique history and interests and responses to situations. And, most of all, a person who, as a museum professional, can explain those responses–both the personal and the universal–in terms that your colleagues can understand and discuss. Every visitor, like you, will have his or her own experience. But among visitors there are emergent patterns of responses that have been formally studied and published, and those constitute a body of knowledge about visitors that you, as a museum professional, know about.

By placing the practitioner in the role of visitor, the Framework asks users to record and reflect upon their actual experiences in an exhibition including their emotional responses to the exhibition and how aspects of it influenced their experience. In this way, museum professionals focus on the experience using affect over intellectual language in their Call-outs.

Definition of "Visitors"

By "visitors" we mean culturally diverse people who are spending leisure time, are curiosity-driven, have no specialized prior knowledge, are likely to have a social agenda, might be in an intergenerational group, who desire engaging experiences, need and appreciate orientation, might be first-timers to the museum, are time-limited, and are ready to learn if it can happen easily and quickly.

Not "the Visitor's Perspective"

The phrase "the visitor's perspective," which is what some of our peers thought we were saying, implies that we have spoken to visitors and are reporting what they said, or what we observed them say or do in the exhibition we were judging. That is not what we did. That's research or evaluation, which is an indispensable part of any exhibit process. We aren't trying to read visitors' minds. We are reading our own minds, viewing the exhibit through our own eyes, and reporting our own reactions to the experience.

It may seem like a subtle distinction, but it's a crucial one. We are not assessing the visitors; we are assessing the

If I were trying to name this something unambiguous, I would lean towards something more like the "exhibit-experience perspective." To me, the word "experience" already captures the sense of someone walking through a completed installation and responding to all the elements that make it work as it does. I don't yet see an elegant way to use the word "visitor" without implying that you're trying to step into their shoes.

Lisa Hubbell

The part that I like best about the Framework is that it provides a vocabulary for talking about the "visitor experience." It renders the term "visitor experience" more concrete because one can discuss it in terms of four large categories—comfort, engagement, reinforcing, meaning—and also in terms of the more specific Criteria for each category.

Gretchen Jennings

exhibits and ourselves. We are not recording what the visitors do; we are looking at what opportunities the exhibits afford. Audience research might report, "Visitors were highly engaged, spending an average of 35 minutes in the gallery." An Excellent Judges discussion group might report, "The exhibition contained a lot of engaging features, components with interesting and challenging activities, and some were open-ended."

Perhaps an analogy would help. If someone offered an exhibit critique "from an educator's perspective," you would expect the author to be an educator. On the other hand, if she presents her critique as representing "an educational perspective," that's broader. It can include anyone (curator, exhibitor, administrator, teacher, student) who takes educational values to heart and uses those values to structure her statements. Thus, to say we are taking "a visitor-centered perspective" means we are framing our critique not around what happened in the design studio or the research lab, but around what happens for visitors on the gallery floor. But how do we do that?

Movie critic Gene Siskel once said that when he went to see a movie, he had two people in his head. One was just a guy, a member of the audience, responding to the movie like anyone else—laughing, crying, anxious, whatever. But at the same time, the other half of his head was the critic asking, "Why?" What is happening in this movie that makes me react this way? Or, if the movie is bad, why is it failing to move me? Another movie critic, Roger Ebert, says "It's not what the film is about. It's how it's about what it's about." This perspective helps distance the critic from the content itself (your love of—or distaste for—the subject) and see what the experiencing of it was.

With the EJ Framework, we try to take the same approach to exhibits. We react to the experience in our own personal, idiosyncratic way. But we also observe our reactions and try to identify which exhibit features caused them.

What we are asking is, What's in it for the visitor? Based on decades of visitor studies, educational theory, and behavioral research, we can recognize what is likely to afford positive learning experiences for visitors. There's a difference, of course, between saying something is "likely" to happen and saying that it did. Evaluation with actual visitor feedback is necessary to establish whether or not learning actually did take place. (See comparisons between assessing exhibitions with the Framework versus other forms of reviewing on pages 91 to 106.)

I do think it's possible for a group of trained judges to identify at least the major strengths and weaknesses of exhibitions from a visitor perspective, in the sense that using a combination of personal response and knowledge of visitor studies principles is likely to lead to a reasonably successful prediction of actual visitor responses. And I think the tool is particularly helpful for guiding our attention to key Aspects of an exhibition that we may otherwise overlook. Obviously, it can never be a substitute for evaluation studies grounded in data about visitor use and interpretation, which I see as the ultimate arbiter in cases of disagreement.

Sue Allen

Presenting the Framework as a summation of "what research says" is certainly valuable. But asking museum professionals to represent the visitor's perspective, based on that expertise, risks falling into the very kinds of assumptions that the visitor studies field exists to question.

Lisa Hubbell

How Design Fits into the Framework

Eugene Dillenburg contributed to this chapter.

Design is an integral part of the exhibition environment for the overall visitor experience. Several of the Excellent Judges (EJ) developers were designers, and they are comfortable that their contributions to an exhibition are reflected in the way the Criteria and Aspects are written and assessed.

Everything on the exhibit floor is your responsibility. You're even accountable for what you choose to leave out. It's your job to anticipate how the audience will use the exhibit and to anticipate what they will want to know about the topic and when they will want it. You have to meet or exceed visitor expectations. If you don't, no matter how understandable the excuse, you didn't fulfill your responsibility.

Don Hughes

The EJ Framework was developed specifically for interpretive exhibitions–those that attempt to convey some educational content or message to the visitors. The four Criteria–Comfortable, Engaging, Reinforcing, and Meaningful–address issues of design as they are embedded in the exhibitions and contribute to the visitor's experience. When the judges use the Framework during an exhibit visit, they write specific notes about their reactions to the designed environment. So the short answer to the question, "Does the Framework consider design features?" is definitely "Yes."

Some exhibit designers have told us that the framework's focus on things to do (e.g., reading, engaging with interactive elements, noticing intellectual integrity) gave short shrift to crucial design issues. The Framework was written admittedly with content-driven science exhibitions in mind and its language is that of the interpretive developer.

What an Exhibit Designer Told Us

In the last year or so of the project, as we were field-testing a version of the Framework, we heard from a designer who felt the tool wasn't adequately addressing his concerns. Bart Hays, then at the Science Museum of Minnesota, was perhaps our most eloquent critic:

> Design is a problem-solving art. The problem to solve is how to create an environment that supports the content, is consistent with the intent of development, and keeps visitor experience as the top priority. When I look at the visitor experience, I can backtrack and see how design did influence it, for good or for ill. Design affects everything.

> However, I feel, the bulk of the language [in the tool] serves the interest of developers, and that's fine. I can learn a great deal from evaluating how the content and structure of an exhibit works, and by engaging in a conversation with my peers about it. My personal opinion was that I could have had a more meaningful conversation about issues that directly relate to my role if there was more design language in the Framework.

Design does affect everything. Color, light, material, shape, sound–all have a tremendous effect on the exhibit experience. And the Framework emphasizes experience: your affective reaction to what is presented, rather than your intellectual analysis of what is presented. Since design elements are a big part of any exhibit experience, they will naturally have a great influence on your reactions and thus on how you assess the exhibits. The designers who helped develop the Framework felt that, due to this emphasis on experience, it can't help but encompass design, even without being a checklist of specific design features.

Judges' "Call-Outs" Respond Directly to Design Features

Design-centered features are likely to show up as Call-outs when judges visit an exhibition: "I was impressed by the dramatic lighting." "The dark color on the walls made me feel claustrophobic." The Framework provides a regulated means to describe the exhibit experience at the immediate affective level. Call-outs such as these demonstrate how design influenced that experience, for better or for worse, and the Call-outs are the basis for noting the Aspects and rating the Criteria. In this way, design is indeed fully integrated into the Framework, from the bottom up.

I look at the design and ask: Does it push the content without being decorative? Does the design keep referring me back to the main messages of the exhibit? I want continuity and consistency from the design.

Don Hughes

The Framework is about design because it focuses on how the exhibits presented the messages, not so much on what the messages were. But while it is fairly content-neutral, the Framework places a good deal of emphasis on meaning, and to some people "meaning" is understood as "facts." But even here design plays a crucial role–not just in presenting content, but in actually creating it. Frank Madsen, an independent designer who was part of the EJ team, cited a number of ways in which design builds meaning:

> Immersive environments and other stage-setting design obviously make a direct contribution to exhibit content. But there are subtler effects, too. Simply having an exhibit that is beautifully designed and built means the exhibit team cared. They considered the topic important enough to merit their best work. More importantly, it means they respect the visitors, and think they deserve the best, too. Such effort works, however subconsciously, to welcome and engage visitors and make them receptive to the content.

Graphic design also plays a role. Comfort and meaning are reinforced, not just through carefully crafted words, but also through legible typeface, contextual placement, and other visual clues. Good design engages visitors, making them ready and willing to experience more.

The Role of Intention

Contributors to this chapter include Barbara Becker and Eugene Dillenburg.

In her essay, "Intention Does Count" (NAME *Exhibitionist*, Vol. 21, No. 2, Fall 2002), Marlene Chambers challenged some of the ideas put forth in the publication of our first efforts ("A Tool for Judging Excellence in Museum Exhibitions") in the *Exhibitionist* (Spring 2001) and in our first American Association of Museums conference panel discussion in the spring of 2002. In the intervening months, we had considered many of the same issues to which Chambers brought her attention and had drawn many of the same conclusions.

Of Course Intentions Count

The title of Chambers' article refers to a statement we made during our panel session at the AAM 2002 annual meeting that "intent doesn't matter." But whose intentions are being referred to? An exhibit maker's, an outside critic's, the visitors', or ours–the users of the Framework?

The intentions we are not paying attention to are those that exist in the minds of the exhibit makers. We do not ask the institution, "What were your objectives for this exhibition? What were you trying to communicate or accomplish? What was your educational intent?" If, on the other hand, the exhibition's intentions are clearly communicated to visitors in the exhibition itself, then of course we consider them, as any other visitor might reflect on them.

Visitors' intentions also obviously matter, as they have informed the very core of our Criteria. Visitors' needs, expectations, and fundamental prerequisites for meaning-making are primary in our definition of excellence.

The Excellent Judges Framework assesses an exhibition as excellent by the opportunities it creates for visitors to meet their own goals, not by how well the exhibit makers met theirs. The Criteria and Aspects of the Framework are drawn from visitor studies literature about how visitors typically approach, use, think about, and meet challenges in museum exhibitions. By "their own goals" we mean, generally speaking, visitors' expectations to have comfortable, engaging, stimulating, social, meaningful, informal learning experiences in an exhibition. These are the visitors' intentions that the Framework clearly addresses.

Our intention—the point of the Excellent Judges exercise (discussing the Framework ahead of time; visiting the assigned exhibition individually; writing Rationales for our ratings; and meeting as a group to discuss them)—is to improve our professional awareness about what worked in the exhibition from the visitor-centered perspective and about what might have worked better. We believe that discussions like ours can lead to better professionals and ultimately to more excellent exhibitions.

This display afforded a feeling of relevance to the information by including examples of personal statements by local university professors.

I've gone to so many exhibits that were presumably put on by people who thought they were doing a good job only to throw my hands up in disgust at missed opportunities.

Kitty Connolly

35

Doing the Math, or Not

Having separate rubrics for each Criterion and the Aspects highlights differences of judgment and still sparks productive discussions among judges.

Matt Sikora

Chambers doubted that we could reach consensus in our assessments. One of the challenges of our research was to see what level of reliability was possible. As we refined our Criteria, we achieved more agreement about what aspects of excellence are important, and the final draft of the Framework represented consensus for the Criteria and their Aspects. But interpreting the Criteria is a more highly variable endeavor. (This is discussed more in the chapter Issues of Validity and Reliability, in Part IV.)

Even without close agreements among judges, our discussions have high value because the process of judging reveals different Rationales behind people's thinking. Now we're talking with each other instead of at each other, and our disagreements may be more interesting than any consensus we reach. Mathematical precision is not our goal, and we dropped the earlier 20-point scoring system in favor of a rubric that emphasizes Rationales rather than ratings, observations and descriptions over numbers.

No Satisfaction

We eliminated the use of "satisfaction" as one of the Criteria for excellence in exhibitions because measures of satisfaction appear to be best observed outside of the exhibition itself: Does the visitor buy something from the shop? Tell friends about the exhibition? Plan a return visit? In short, satisfaction is an assessment that better describes the visitor than the exhibition. Again, the purpose of the Framework is to assess opportunities–what the exhibits afford–not to judge the visitors themselves.

Articles such as Chambers' tested our thinking, clarified our conversations, and helped us to reexamine our intentions. And we certainly agree with much of what she said. For example, "Translating the findings of museum researchers into excellent exhibitions is the trick. There's no doubt, though, that what we are learning about the visitor's intentions and the affective aspects of her museum experience has already profoundly influenced the intentions of many exhibition developers" (Chambers 2002).

PART III

HOW TO USE THE FRAMEWORK

The Excellent Judges Framework has five steps in the process of assessing excellence in exhibitions: 1. The First Meeting; 2. Creating Call-outs; 3. Assessing the Aspects; 4. Rating the Criteria; and 5. The Second Meeting. These are explained in the worksheets, reproduced on the next six pages, and described in greater detail in the text following them. To see a snippet of what an Excellent Judges meeting and a walk-though of an exhibition by a judge look like, play the 6-minute video on the CD. These five steps apply to using the Framework for professional development among a group of peers. There are other uses as well: as a teaching tool; as a formative evaluation or exhibit planning tool; as a model for creating other standards for judging excellence; or as a personal reminder of how to be more visitor-centered. These applications are discussed elsewhere.

The worksheets here are ready
to be photocopied and used.

The forms are also available
in two larger formats,
downloadable from
the CD.

FRAMEWORK

Assessing Excellence in Exhibitions from a Visitor-Centered Perspective

Use this Framework to talk with your peers about excellence
and improve your professional practice.

❶
First Meeting

Gather a team of six to 10 museum professionals and meet for at least two hours to
become familiar with the Framework and to come to a common understanding of
procedures before judging an exhibition.

You will be rating and discussing an exhibition regarding its level of achievement for
four different **Criteria**. Is the exhibition:

Comfortable? Engaging? Reinforcing? Meaningful?

1. Comfortable

An excellent exhibition helps the visitor feel comfortable—physically and psychologically.
Good comfort opens the door to other positive experiences. Lack of comfort prevents them.

2. Engaging

An excellent exhibition is engaging for visitors. It entices them to pay attention.
Engagement is the first step toward finding meaning.

3. Reinforcing

In an excellent exhibition, the exhibits provide visitors with abundant opportunities to be
successful and to feel intellectually competent—beyond the "wow" of engagement.
In addition, the exhibits reinforce each other, providing multiple means of accessing similar
bits of information that are all part of a cohesive whole. Visitors are confidently on their way
to having meaningful experiences.

4. Meaningful

An excellent exhibition provides personally relevant experiences for visitors. Beyond being
engaged and feeling competent, visitors find themselves changed, cognitively and affectively,
in immediate and long-lasting ways.

Ratings are based on two different kinds of data:

> **Call-outs:** your experiences in the exhibition as a visitor
> **Aspects:** the evidence you found that supported each Criterion

At the end of the first meeting, pick an exhibition to visit.

Exhibition Title _____

Institution _____ Your Initials _____ _____ Date of Visit _____

Create Call-Outs

Visit the exhibition by yourself. Keep notes about your experience in the form of sentences with feeling verbs—your thoughts, feelings and responses as you experience the exhibition as a visitor. These are your Call-outs.

❸
Assess the Aspects

After visiting, leave the exhibition and then assess the Aspects—the evidence defining each Criterion—listed below. Using your Call-outs as a reference, think about to what degree each Aspect was appropriately present or not present in the exhibition. Using the following guidelines, put pluses and minuses in the right-hand columns.

++ Excellent, a wonderful example	— Not quite there	**NA** Does not apply (Not all Aspects
+ A good example	— — Self-defeating	apply to all exhibitions.)

1. Aspects of Comfortable

a. Physical and conceptual orientation devices were present.	
b. There were convenient places to rest.	
c. The lighting, temperature, and sound levels were appropriate.	
d. Everything was well-kept, functioning, and in good repair.	
e. There was a good ergonomic fit. Exhibit elements could be read, viewed and used with ease.	
f. Choices and options for things to do were clear. Visitors were encouraged to feel in control of their own experiences.	
g. Authorship, biases, intent, and perspectives of the exhibition were revealed, identified, or attributed. The exhibits reveal who is talking, fact from fiction or opinion, the real from the not real.	
h. The exhibition welcomed people of different cultural backgrounds, economic classes, educational levels, and physical abilities.	

2. Aspects of Engaging

a. The physical environment looked interesting and invited exploration.	
b. Exhibits caught my attention and enticed me to slow down, to look, interact, and spend time attending to many elements.	
c. Exhibits were fun—pleasurable, challenging, amusing, intriguing, and intellectually or physically stimulating.	
d. Exhibit components encouraged and promoted social behaviors. Exhibits encouraged visitors to call one another over, read out loud, point at, and converse about the exhibit material.	
e. Experiences came in a variety of formats (e.g., graphics, text, objects, AV, computers, living things, models, phenomena) and a variety of sensory modalities—sight, sound, motion, touch, etc..	
f. Regardless of a visitor's prior knowledge or interests, there were interesting things to do.	

3. Aspects of Reinforcing

a. The exhibition was not overwhelming. There were "just enough" things to do.	
b. Challenging or complex exhibit experiences were structured so that visitors who tried to figure them out were likely to say, "I got it," and feel confident and motivated to do more.	
c. The presentation had a logic. It held together intellectually in a way that was easily followed and understood.	
d. The information and ideas in different parts of the exhibition were complementary and reinforced each other.	
e. The exhibit built on itself.	

4. Aspects of Meaningful

a. Ideas and objects in the exhibition (natural specimens, living collections, cultural artifacts, demonstrations, and activities) were made relevant to and easily integrated into the visitors' experience, regardless of their levels of knowledge or motivation.	
b. The exhibition made a case that its content had value. The material was timely, important, and resonated with the visitors' values. Meaning is the "so what."	
c. The exhibition content touched on universal human concerns and didn't shy away from deep or controversial issues.	
d. The exhibit experience promoted change in people's thinking and feeling, even transcendence. Exhibits gave visitors the means to make generalizations, change beliefs and attitudes, and/or take action.	

❹
Rate the Criteria

To what extent did you think each Criterion was likely to be experienced in the exhibition?

Assign a rating level (1-6) to each Criterion.

Level 1 Excellent—Consistently good Aspects (+'s), with many excellent (++'s)
Level 2 Very Good—Consistently good Aspects (+'s) with very few or no misses (−'s)
Level 3 Good—Mostly good Aspects (+'s), but with some misses (−'s)
Level 4 Acceptable—A balance between good Aspects (+'s) and missed Aspects (−'s), or a few noteworthy things
Level 5 Misses Opportunities—Mostly missed Aspects (−'s), but there may be a few good Aspects (+'s)
Level 6 Counterproductive—Mostly self-defeating (− −'s), with many missed Aspects (−'s)

Using the evidence of your Call-outs and Aspects, write a Rationale for your rating.

1. Comfortable

Level   Rationale:

2. Engaging

Level   Rationale:

3. Reinforcing

Level   Rationale:

4. Meaningful

Level   Rationale:

❺
Assessment Comparison Meeting

Allow at least two hours for the follow-up meeting. Start by recording everyone's ratings in the chart below.

Criteria Level Ratings Summary

Judge's Initials	Comfortable	Engaging	Reinforcing	Meaningful
1.				
2.				
3.				
4.				
5.				
6.				
7.				
8.				
9.				
10.				

Any Strong Disagreements?
Discuss areas of greatest disagreement among the ratings above. Why do you disagree?

Recording Consensus
Discuss, then list, specific features, experiences, or feelings about the exhibition—
both positive and negative—that you ALL agree on.

1. _____
2. _____
3. _____
4. _____
5. _____

Social Moderation
After all the discussions, did anyone want to modify their ratings? If so, alter the ratings in the chart above.

Congratulations! You are now an Excellent Judge!

This project was supported in part by the National Science Foundation.
Opinions expressed are those of the authors and not necessarily those of the Foundation.

1. The First Meeting–Orientation

The purpose of the first meeting is to get everyone together and to develop a shared understanding of the language of the Framework, getting to know what the words "Criteria," "Aspects," "Call-outs," and "Rationales" mean. Peers, coworkers, and/or students meet to discuss the vocabulary and the process and to go over the steps of using the Framework. Depending on the type of group that gets together and people's experience with the Framework, the start of the meeting will vary:

- If the group consists of all in-house staff or museum studies students together in a class, the participants will already know each other, and one person might be the appointed leader.

- If the group consists of peers from different institutions in the same city, the introductory meeting will help people get to know who is around the table and who to expect to see again at the second meeting. There does not need to be a leader.

If group members have used the Framework together before, the meeting will probably begin with people catching up with what others have been doing.

Having a group of at least six people makes for an interesting diversity of opinions and discussions, especially later in the process. More than 10 people will probably be less manageable, so the ideal number is between six and 10.

While selecting a leader isn't essential, the group can benefit from having someone responsible for keeping everyone on task. People have a tendency to drift into purely social conversation, while the point of using the Framework is to talk more deeply and thoughtfully, which takes more concentrated and directed effort.

For groups meeting for the first time, people can share their understanding of what the Framework is and how it works. Questions might range from, "Who funded this? Is the Framework used for finished exhibitions or ones under development?" to "What does a 'visitor-centered perspective' mean?" Some people might be familiar with an earlier version of the Framework (from information published in 2001), not the improved Criteria and format developed in 2004. For example:

JUDGE 1: *Do the Aspects add up to the whole, or is there is a subjective opinion as well?*

JUDGE 2: *It's like rating science fairs, where you can have a subjective opinion (overall rating), but when you add up the marks on all the details (Aspects) it might come out very differently.*

JUDGE 1: *So both are important.*

As the group discusses the layout and definitions of the Framework, other questions might arise, such as, "Does 'reinforcing' mean you or the exhibition? Is it necessary for everyone to fill in the last page before the second meeting? Will the museum staff members whose exhibition it was see these comments?" People who have read this book and know the answers can assist others.

When our last group of EJ group met in Chicago to test one of the final iterations of the Framework, they noticed that there were similarities with the Framework's Criteria and process and other fields, such as retail marketing or art fair judging. They speculated what it would be like if everyone agreed on something or if they were "all over the map" on some items. They realized that doing the Framework process is hard work, and it takes a commitment of time and effort to do it right.

These first discussions will clarify for participants three important concepts: (1) the Call-outs are written in your own language, from your own feelings and perspectives while you are visiting the exhibition; (2) the Criteria and Aspects are the shared language that the Framework gives the group; and (3) assessing the Aspects on the basis of your Call-outs is a bridge between the two. It is important for everyone to see how the Call-outs work from a direct-experience, bottom-up approach, while the Criteria are top-down.

Participants should also notice that the Criteria and Aspects are written in positive language: These are desired Criteria and positive Aspects found in an excellent exhibition experience. When judging and assessing, it's hard to think positively. It's easier to pick out what didn't work, so the Framework is set up to get people to think—for the purpose of best practices—of what is good.

When people are feeling comfortably familiar with the Framework and don't have any questions left to discuss, it is time to ask, What exhibition should we visit? And, When should we schedule the second group meeting? No one should leave the first group meeting without a thorough understanding of how the Framework form is to be used in the exhibition. If they don't, their participation in the second group meeting will not be on the same wavelength as the others. The Framework facilitates group discussions with a shared vocabulary, and the first meeting is meant to firmly establish that language.

It's good to allow at least three weeks between the first and second meeting, so people have ample time to fit the exhibit visit into their schedules.

Selecting the Exhibition to Visit

Peer or student groups should use these factors for selecting the exhibition: It should be in a museum open to the public with regular hours; be accessible by public transportation (for those who don't have a car); have affordable admission charges; and not be a traveling show. The last criterion is important because a temporary exhibition might not be up long enough for everyone to get to it. And often there are reasons to revisit or send other people to verify or check out what you experienced, or get a photograph of an exemplar.

The Framework is most appropriately used with exhibitions that have a clear didactic intent, that is, they are meant to be educational experiences for a broad range of ages and abilities (it is less useful at art exhibitions without any interpretive content or children's exhibits meant for focused play only). We visited exhibitions at natural history, cultural history, science, and art museums. Museums with living collections (zoos, aquariums, botanical gardens) have exhibitions that are easy to review with the Framework. An example of the decision-making process of an EJ group in Chicago, where different people were more or less familiar with what the local institutions had on display, went along these lines:

JUDGE 1: *How about something at the Mexican Museum of Fine Arts?*

JUDGE 2: *I think they're undergoing remodeling.*

JUDGE 3: *How about* Eternal Egypt *at Field? At the Field we know the exhibition will be quality.*

JUDGE 4: *Yeah, but that's a traveling exhibition. We should pick something permanent.*

JUDGE 5: *Does the Shedd Aquarium do "real" exhibits, or do they just have animals on display?*

JUDGE 3: *Sure they do.* Wild Reef *is new at Shedd.*

JUDGE 2: *Do we all have to do the same exhibition?*

JUDGE 4: *Yes, according to the Framework.*

JUDGE 2: *Do we go as a group?*

JUDGE 4: *No, it says "visit the exhibition on your own."*

2. Creating Call-Outs

The judges each visit the exhibition on their own, during public hours. They take the Framework with them and write Call-outs (on page 2 of the form) while they walk around and at the end of the experience. They can take as long as they want. Some people do it all in one pass; others walk through the exhibition several times. It's up to the individual.

Just what is a "Call-out"? And how do I write it? It's a big component of that orientation and getting yourself in the mindset of using feeling words. Not.... "I hated that thing," but "I found the orientation map was successful because...." And trying to get that vocabulary down. I think that's part of why it takes so much time to get comfortable and to have that shared technique for visiting.

Nancy Owens Renner

Call-outs are written spontaneously, as affective statements–your feelings and emotional reactions to what you are experiencing–along with some analysis for why or what made you feel that way. Writing them on the Framework form puts the Call-outs in a place that is easy to refer to later, when you're thinking about your ratings and Rationales.

Below are examples of Call-outs, all for *The Swamp* at Brookfield Zoo– an indoor, immersive walk-through habitat with water, cypress trees, Spanish moss, and boardwalks. Many of the exhibits these Call-outs refer to can be seen on the 6-minute video on the CD. The CD photo captions contain more Call-outs.

Good intro/layout sign—tells me what to expect and where; satisfies my craving for orientation. Shows that I will be entering and exiting through different doorways, in a one-way traffic pattern. I like getting a preview of what's going on, and it shows me what I'll see and how it's laid out. I feel comfortable and relaxed knowing this as I go in, through the right-hand door.

Sign says, "What swamps are good for" right away. Counters the stereotype of swamps being dismal and worthless.

Floor in here is surprisingly squishy and soft, not hard. But it smells like bird-poop. That's not too nice, but it's a zoo after all. I see live birds up ahead. There are big cypress trees with moss, fake? I guess they are.

Graphic of the "knees" of a cypress tree. Explains what knees are, satisfies my curiosity clearly. It shows how they are connected to the tree under-water. I never realized that.

There are short signs near the snakes. I like snakes, and I like short snake signs; they're easy and quick to read, and the information relates to what I can see, even though the snake is sleeping.

Boardwalk is a change of floor surface, which helps signal me that I am entering a different area of the exhibition, another orientation clue.

Another change in the floor surface, two steps up, and banners overhead—"Swamp Fest"—Another change of pace

Push button to hear the gator's bellow. There's a quote and a picture too. I enjoy the combination of the real animal, the recorded sound, the poetic quote, and the artistic picture. Lots of different ways to access the information.

Big alligator. Is it alive? Yes! It moved. How lucky to see that.

Case with graphics and objects that confirm stereotype of the evil swamp concept—with humor, but by now I've been entertained and intrigued more than I've been scared.

Here are lots of facts, objects, and photographs of people who have lived in the swamp—Cajuns, Seminoles, and the people who used to live in the Okefenokee Swamp. Push buttons to hear examples of their songs. Okefenokees have a really weird yodel. There's lots of stuff here, maybe too much. It feels busy, overloaded, not aesthetically presented.

Turning the big panel makes beads drop through two channels. One side represents a swamp with lots of plants that slow down the flow. I'm not sure everyone would get this, but it's sure fun to turn the panel and listen to the sound of the beads flowing through.

Push this button and it shows me what happens if swamps are eliminated. Surprise—Floating furniture! I like the humor.

Kids are jumping in and out of the boat for the Swamp Boat Ride video. The video sign says it lasts four minutes. Guess I could sit and rest for that long. It's not narrated, but it has

natural background sounds. I like to see a video that doesn't demand that I listen to someone talk at me. Gives me some space to hear my own thoughts.

Through some swinging screen doors into another section, like a saw mill. Little jewel boxes of small animals up close along one wall.

A big cypress tree trunk cross section tells me what was going on way back when the tree was alive. This is a history lesson in a zoo! Very interdisciplinary! Poor planning to have a bench right in front of it.

Kids are pulling the crayfish trap up out of the water. Pretty simple activity, but they seem to line up to get the chance to do it. More good whole-body kinesthetic for kids.

"Birds need rest stops too" and there's a duck resting. But he's got nowhere to go now. An interactive map nearby shows migration routes—series of lights indicate pathways; long distances, some over water. I am impressed with the birds' adaptations.

The Illinois wetland area has the ever-popular otters; these are freshwater river otters. They're beautiful and so active. Engaging to watch them swim.

These little mini-diorama boxes light up inside when you push the button for a little scene showing a conservation message. Simple, cute, to the point, and much more engaging than just preachy text.

I've spent more than 20 minutes in here, because I was stopping, looking, and reading more often than most other visitors were doing. Most people gave their attention to the animals. Between live animals and all other objects, photos, videos, or labels, animals always win.

Overall this was really enjoyable, engaging, surprising, and both serious and fun. The immersion really worked for me, although in places it got crowded. My attitude about swamps has been improved: I appreciate them more.

The Call-outs are core to the process. The protocol and Framework format promote attention to them. Do not ignore or skip!

Barbara Becker

Call-outs are written without making any structured reference to the Aspects or the Criteria. You write them as you feel them. After going through the exhibition, you might want to sit down and go over them again, clarifying your thoughts and feelings, adding some others, fleshing out some of the details. The Call-outs will provide the basis for assessing the Aspects and writing Rationales, although there is not necessarily a one-to-one ratio. Many Call-outs will apply to more than one Aspect or Criteria.

3. Assessing the Aspects

Page 3 of the Framework lists the Aspects for each Criterion. As you read each one, think about your Call-outs. Was there evidence in your concrete experiences for any of the Aspects noted for each Criteria? Write a plus for every Aspect that you have positive evidence for. Put multiple pluses if there were wonderful examples of the Aspect; put a minus if the Aspects were weak, missing, or self-defeating. Put "NA" if the Aspect does not apply to the exhibition you just visited. Not all Aspects need to be found in every exhibition.

There are no "zero" or neutral ratings for the Aspects because the evidence is either working for the Aspect or against it. Even though some elements may seem to be "just for mood" or as "set decoration," nothing in an exhibition is neutral or "not really part of it."

Some judges like to do this step immediately after their visit; others prefer to wait and reflect later. The advantage to doing the plus-minus ratings right away is that if you have a question about a detail, you can go back and check it. Note, however, that this step is not best accomplished while walking through the exhibition–that's the best time to write your Call-outs. You wait to assess Aspects later because it is a reflective, holistic process, not a concrete checklist. You need to see all of the evidence (i.e., the whole exhibition) before you can assess the Aspects fairly. The evidence (positive and negative) for each Aspect may come from different places in the exhibition.

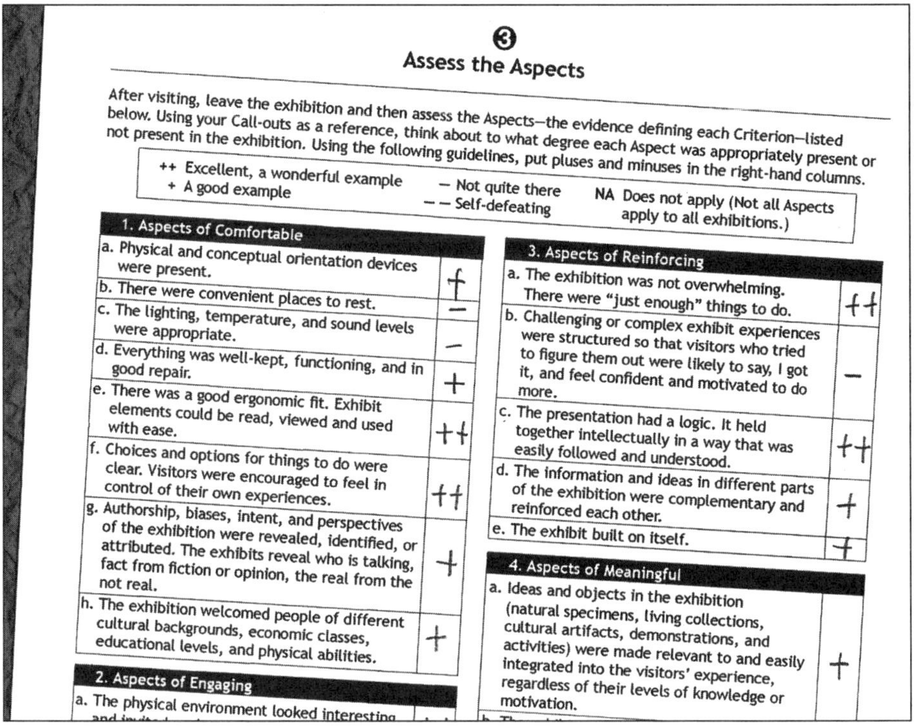

❸ Assess the Aspects

After visiting, leave the exhibition and then assess the Aspects—the evidence defining each Criterion—listed below. Using your Call-outs as a reference, think about to what degree each Aspect was appropriately present or not present in the exhibition. Using the following guidelines, put pluses and minuses in the right-hand columns.

++ Excellent, a wonderful example
+ A good example
− Not quite there
− − Self-defeating
NA Does not apply (Not all Aspects apply to all exhibitions.)

1. Aspects of Comfortable

a. Physical and conceptual orientation devices were present.	
b. There were convenient places to rest.	+
c. The lighting, temperature, and sound levels were appropriate.	−
d. Everything was well-kept, functioning, and in good repair.	−
e. There was a good ergonomic fit. Exhibit elements could be read, viewed and used with ease.	+
f. Choices and options for things to do were clear. Visitors were encouraged to feel in control of their own experiences.	++
	++
g. Authorship, biases, intent, and perspectives of the exhibition were revealed, identified, or attributed. The exhibits reveal who is talking, fact from fiction or opinion, the real from the not real.	+
h. The exhibition welcomed people of different cultural backgrounds, economic classes, educational levels, and physical abilities.	+

2. Aspects of Engaging

a. The physical environment looked interesting	

3. Aspects of Reinforcing

a. The exhibition was not overwhelming. There were "just enough" things to do.	++
b. Challenging or complex exhibit experiences were structured so that visitors who tried to figure them out were likely to say, I got it, and feel confident and motivated to do more.	−
c. The presentation had a logic. It held together intellectually in a way that was easily followed and understood.	++
d. The information and ideas in different parts of the exhibition were complementary and reinforced each other.	+
e. The exhibit built on itself.	+

4. Aspects of Meaningful

a. Ideas and objects in the exhibition (natural specimens, living collections, cultural artifacts, demonstrations, and activities) were made relevant to and easily integrated into the visitors' experience, regardless of their levels of knowledge or motivation.	+

A truly excellent exhibition will have multiple examples of evidence for all Aspects and all Criteria.

For examples of how Call-outs can be related to rating the Aspects, see the photo captions on the CD.

Unless it is an exhibit about decoration, don't decorate. It obscures meaning.

Frank Madsen

4. Rating the Criteria

Some people wait until the day before the meeting to visit the assigned exhibition and fill in the worksheets. Others prefer to have at least a few days to think through their experience before completing the assessments. Either way, people should fill out the rating levels and Rationales on the Framework before coming to the second group meeting. They should have carefully thought through their own choices and reasons before they are possibly influenced by others in the group.

To assign ratings and write Rationales, look back over your pluses and minuses on the Aspects page, then reflect on the overall evidence for each Criterion. To what extent were Criteria supported? Did you experience or see evidence for affording their Aspects? You will rate each Criterion: Level 1 is the highest, and Level 6 is the lowest.

In the examples below of Rationales for ratings of "Good" (Level 3) for Criteria–from a different judge in different exhibitions–notice how they draw on the language of the Aspects:

LEVEL 3 FOR COMFORT in *Underground Adventure* at the Field Museum

A few ergonomic flaws, such as bad sightlines for kids, but a good fit spatially. Things were well-lit and I found places to sit when I needed them. Had

the obligatory cross-cultural people graphics. Navigation was a challenge in a couple of spots. Like the Mud Room.

LEVEL 3 FOR REINFORCING in *Wild Reef*
at Shedd Aquarium

All the content built on itself and reinforced what I had just learned. I think it could have been integrated better as far as the cultural subject matter to provide a more cohesive picture between the animals and the people on the coral reef.

LEVEL 3 FOR MEANINGFUL in *Statue of an Emperor*
at the Getty Museum

Ideas were made relevant and surprisingly easy to understand although I can't say I felt an effort to integrate the visitor into the experience in terms of 'daily life' connections, cultural relevancy, or larger issues of conservation. Learning about the statue's past, survival, and preservation was a topic of appeal to me, and I appreciated the behind-the-scenes peeks into the process. Some of the content required an assumed knowledge level, for example geography. Overall interesting although not strikingly life-changing.

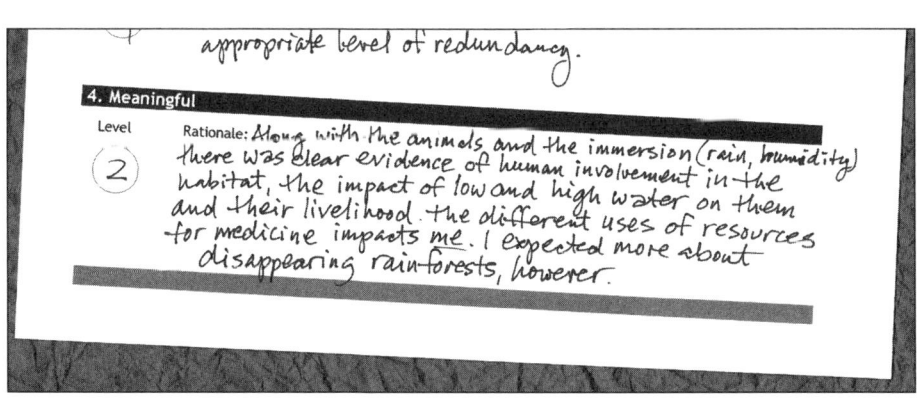

appropriate level of redundancy.

4. Meaningful

Level ②

Rationale: Along with the animals and the immersion (rain, humidity) there was clear evidence of human involvement in the habitat, the impact of low and high water on them and their livelihood. the different uses of resources for medicine impacts me. I expected more about disappearing rain-forests, however.

Try not to let one bad experience overshadow your rating for the whole Criterion, although this happens surprisingly easily. Write in the rating level number in the circle provided, and then write your Rationale for the rating. Why did you give it that number? Don't wait to hear what other assessors have said before you decide. Think independently and deeply about your own judgments. You can change your mind later if you want to.

Remember to write your Rationales based on the presence or absence of evidence for the Aspects listed in the Framework. It's important to use this shared list, not just your own opinions about how exhibitions should be designed, because this focus helps keep the group conversation at the second meeting from spinning off into a hashing of personal biases. Instead of assertions of "I liked this" or "I hated that," the discussion will go into more depth.

The two biggest problems to avoid in making ratings are scoring based on your own personal stylistic preferences and focusing only on the negative Aspects of the performance.

5. The Second Meeting—
Assessing and Comparing

At the second meeting, the group sits down together again for about two hours to review, compare, and discuss their assessments. It might be tempting to just start talking casually about what you liked or didn't like in a freewheeling conversation about different elements of the exhibition, but in the long run the discussion will be deeper, longer, and more useful if you use the Framework as a guide and stick to the format in a systematic way.

A good way to start is by filling in the initials of the judges who are taking part in the meeting, and then, one at a time, fill in the ratings for each Criterion by each judge. The rating numbers are easier to discern and fill out on the grid than the words for the ratings

There was one element that wasn't working—the live camera to a peregrine falcon nest. You know, it was one element out of however many, but I was just like, "Oh, it's not working. What a blow!" And it was a reminder to me, going back to my exhibit professional mind, of what a downer that is in the visitor experience. Just to have one of those key elements not working. So it was a wake-up call, and it shifted my whole score from excellent to very good just because of that one element.

Sue Allen

(e.g., "Excellent" "Misses opportunities"), which is why we use both in the summary meeting. Fill in the whole grid for all four Criteria, and then pick the most interesting place to begin the discussion.

Often the liveliest starting point is where judges have big differences in their ratings. For example, under the Criterion for Comfortable, why did one person give it a Level 2 (Very Good) when someone else gave it a Level 6 (Counterproductive)?

Big differences can occur when one judge has had a particularly annoying experience that colors the feeling of comfort for the whole visit. For example, "It was raining, there was no place to put my wet raincoat, and I had to carry it with me the whole time." Another example: "The guard was rude to me, and I didn't feel welcome." When you witness the power of one bad experience and how it shapes the attitude toward the whole visit, it makes you think twice about dismissing a visitor's so-called trivial complaint.

Less dramatic differences in ratings occur frequently, and ratings within two points are considered "agreement." A three-point spread between levels signals some possible strong differences worth probing: "What Call-outs led you to give it that rating? "

As interesting as the differences are, often we hear strong consensus on why people gave similar ratings, for both positive and negative Aspects. When the group calls out many examples of Aspects that are present in the exhibition and agrees on a number of reasons why they rated the Criteria highly, the exhibition has lots of evidence of excellence.

> *Taking part in the Excellent Judges process has been the most effective, least expensive (in time or money) professional development I have ever done. It provides the framework for me to visit other shows I would probably miss, critique them in a predictable and repeatable way so that I can develop criteria for excellence, and generate conversation with colleagues from whom I learn different perspectives.*
>
> Kitty Connolly

Recording Consensus

The final section to fill out on the form records the specifics of the special features, experiences, or feelings about the exhibition, positive or negative, that everyone agreed on. Examples of consensus:

- In *Wild Reef*, judges agreed that the environment and specimens were stunning, and that the Filipino culture needed to be more integrated throughout the exhibition.

- In *Milky Way*, judges agreed that the exhibits made a difficult and distant topic approachable, and that the most engaging, fun, and meaningful elements were the 3-D theater, "spaghettify," and "Viewing the Galaxy."

- In *Play It Safe*, judges agreed that the exhibits offered good and multiple examples of ways to take action for safety, and that there was no overall message that tied exhibits together.

Given that the Framework is designed to emphasize positive Aspects and Criteria, if the group finds it hard to come to consensus on many things they all liked, then chances are, this was an exhibition that didn't show much excellence. Exhibitions are not wholly "good" or "bad." This is not about the "best" or "worst." It's about thinking more carefully and thoroughly about what makes one thing have more evidence of excellence than another and giving museum practitioners ways to strive for exhibitions that will have the most excellence possible.

Sometimes the discussion will lead to "social moderation" of a judge's rating. After hearing the Rationales of other judges, a person might have a new insight that leads him to change his score. We usually go over the grid again at the end of the two hours and specifically ask, "Does anyone want to change his or her levels for any of the Criteria?" Consensus is not the goal, but it is interesting to see if and why people want to change their minds about something.

It would be helpful for judges to know how much a museum uses visitor studies. Exhibit staffers experienced with visitor studies have a toughened hide for constructive criticism, but those newer to the practice might be put on the defensive by the Excellent Judges process. Judges should be sensitive to this when they present their information.

Colleen Blair

At the end of the meeting, pick a new exhibition to visit, and repeat steps 2 through 5. The more times a group uses the process, the better everyone gets at it. There is definitely a learning curve to using the Framework, and with practice, the interactions become more productive and even more fun.

Judges and critics, whether at the podium of the annual museum conference or in the cocktail lounge, are still welcome to give their personal opinions, laden with professional and personal bias, and those thoughts will always be interesting, challenging–and threatening. No one likes to be judged! But the Framework encourages more people to share in the discussion and to guide the conversation with some common language and ground rules.

FAQ: Who does the assessment? How is an EJ group formed?

It depends on its purpose. An institution may name a group to use the Framework, visiting other similar or dissimilar exhibits, for developing a shared vision for a new exhibition of their own. A group of peers can get together with representatives from a variety of institutions for purposes of professional development. Such a group can also be formed to assess exhibits in a consortium of museums. An individual can use it to think more clearly and deeply about the visitor-centered affordances when planning, reviewing, or critiquing an exhibition. It works well as a teaching tool in museum studies classes. See pages 78 to 83 for how the Framework has been used with museum studies students.

FAQ: Who is qualified to be an assessor? Who are the judges?

The first qualification is that an assessor must be a museum professional: a developer, designer, curator, project manager, or other professional who has experience working on exhibitions. People who are younger, older, more- or less-experienced, from any type or size of museum can take part. Students who have studied exhibitions will benefit from the experience and can bring important insights as well.

The more the assessors know about the body of research on learning in informal settings, the more effective they will be. The Bibliography and Part IV: Theoretical Underpinnings contain helpful references.

Used in the Framework's strictest protocol, the second qualification involves going through an orientation meeting with a group of six to 10, and meeting again for the assessment process with them at least once. Do this, and you are an "Excellent Judge." Who are the judges? You and me.

FAQ: How do you guard against bias on the part of judges?

All judges bring their own styles, preferences and perspectives to the process, and the Framework helps them focus on the same issues and questions. Repeated use of the Framework can get people to see their own biases more clearly and become open to moderation as well as be more open to hearing other people's biases without feeling defensive—and even gain new insights or tolerance.

An assessor may have a bias against exhibitions that do not have interactive elements and a prejudice in favor of ones that do. Judges should become aware of their personal certitudes and challenge themselves.

FAQ: What if the people in the assessing group aren't all that excellent themselves?

Things that can contribute to this are: (1) lack of knowledge about visitor studies; (2) refusal to believe the findings (the "not in my museum" or the "my visitors are different" syndrome); (3) unwillingness to follow the format of the Framework; and/or (4) rigid certitude of personal viewpoints or ego that prohibit sharing and listening skills. These can limit the value of any exercise. Anyone who makes an honest effort to go through the Framework process, however, will be exposed to a new, visitor-oriented way of looking at exhibition design. If people at least consider visitor issues in their work, they will become more excellent.

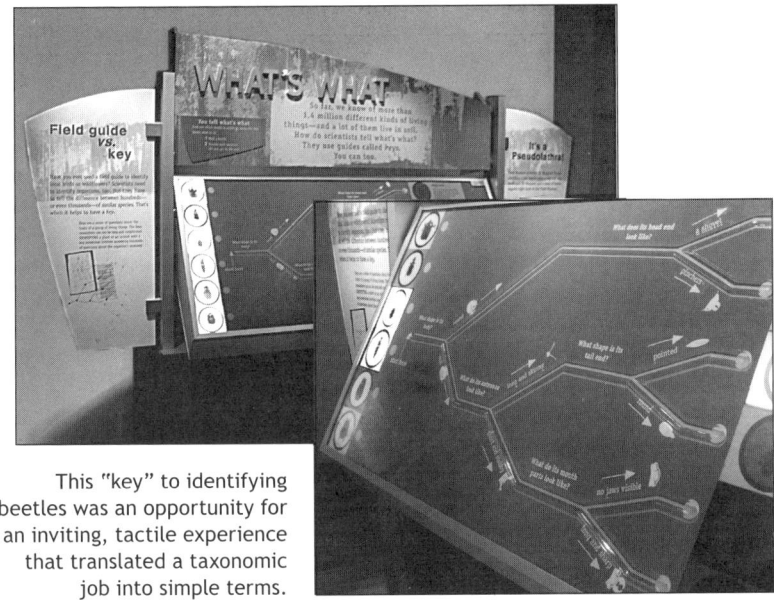

This "key" to identifying beetles was an opportunity for an inviting, tactile experience that translated a taxonomic job into simple terms.

FAQ: Have there been any trends in the ratings so far?

Some tendencies have emerged in the patterns of our ratings of the four Criteria.

- Judges often rated Engagement higher than the other three Criteria.
- Judges often rated Comfort higher than Reinforcement.
- Judges often rated Meaningfulness lowest.

What are the implications of these tendencies? Museums seem to be better at creating exhibitions that are strong in engagement than those with meaningful experiences. You might have already known or suspected that to be true, but the Framework gives exhibit developers some very specific Aspects to think about, either for remediation of an existing exhibition or for making plans for a new one that could be stronger in all four Criteria.

The trend of finding more Aspects of Engagement was witnessed in the selection of photos for this book: It was easier to find examples of engaging exhibit components than reinforcing or meaningful ones.

FAQ: If the goal is discussion rather than a score, why use numeric ratings?

The numbers facilitate conversation. Being asked to give a number score or rating encourages people to take a stand and then defend it. Once areas of disagreement are identified, discussion centers on whether the source is in the exhibit or in the perception of the judges, and whether judges' opinions are open to moderation.

People can surprise you. I've started to think that I can predict how someone will react, and then her feelings about the topic or point of view or lighting level will throw off the whole trajectory. Instead of rating the show based on the haughty labels, a person will rate it based on the wonderful objects. Some patterns are emerging, but slowly. We have one person who is a stickler for correct grammar. Another is more concerned about different learning styles. But we all loved Einstein, so that show ranked high even though it was long, long, long. Go figure.

Kitty Connolly

FAQ: Are there experts that can be brought in to manage the process?

It has been suggested that National Association for Museum Exhibition (NAME, a standing professional committee of the American Association of Museums) organize such workshops, but no ongoing, formal program existed at the time of this publication. Individuals with experience with the Framework may be available on a consulting basis, but the Framework and its protocol are meant for self-organized groups, with or without a leader.

Spending time to visit and thoroughly contemplate exhibitions, followed with those thoughtful discussions with your peers is, unfortunately, seen as a luxury many of us cannot afford.

FAQ: What does it cost to do an assessment?

The main expense is time. The self-guiding Framework forms can be photocopied from this book or downloaded from the CD.

FAQ: What happens with the assessment when it's done?

There's no final report or grade. The point is to have the discussion, not to produce a document. In some cases, however, a summary of the findings of the EJ team were incorporated into a report with other evaluation results. The exhibition's creators may also be given access to the invaluable lists of detailed Call-outs, the Rationales, and/or notes of the assessors' discussion. It's up to the reviewing team and the involvement of the institution being assessed.

What are we going to do with what we heard? We wanted to wait to begin our exhibit remediation until we had this workshop. We can do a lot more with wayfinding and meaning-making.

Charlie Walter and Colleen Blair

FAQ: Isn't it stressful for the people who create an exhibition to be judged this way?

Certainly, it can be uncomfortable to hear criticism. It's important to begin the process (and any reporting about outcomes) by emphasizing that no exhibition is perfect: Every exhibition has strengths and weaknesses. The goal of the Framework process is to identify these, it is not to judge the people who created the exhibition.

Self-assessment, of course, will be welcomed by individuals and institutions struggling to reach excellence. Many institutions already seek peer review. A formal Framework shared across a variety of museums will strengthen their confidence in the outcome.

Being openly critical can be uncomfortable for the judges as well, and the EJ meetings will be most productive when sparks create energy but not fire. Truly Excellent Judges will watch group dynamics and take care to communicate in a positive form.

We hear that the Excellent Judges are coming to Texas. We get really scared. Not really, because at the Fort Worth Museum of Science and History, we know every exhibition we put on the floor has strengths and weaknesses, and everything we do can be made better.

Charlie Walter and Colleen Blair

What if a group of Excellent Judges visits your exhibition and finds some less-than-excellent experiences? How does that impact your status and job? Who is willing to invite such criticism?

How did it feel to be judged? Frankly, first of all, we felt very vulnerable. We had no idea who was judging us. What was their expertise? Secondly, we felt very connected to the field at large. We're always asking ourselves, "How can we contribute to what's going on out there?" And third, at the end of the day, we felt good about it. We'd heard a wide range in the feedback, and there were no big surprises.

Charlie Walter and Colleen Blair

The Biggest Drawbacks

Probably the largest stumbling block for museum professionals using the Framework is to coordinate getting together with five other people. In one's busy schedule, who has the time?

There's no getting around the fact that some people may not feel this exercise is important enough to make time for. They may feel they know it all already. Experienced exhibit developers probably do know the importance of comfort, engagement, reinforcement, and meaningfulness for visitors. But they won't know what they don't know if they don't take the opportunity to engage in professional conversations that encourage them to think differently—by listening to what others think, especially when the other person doesn't necessarily agree with them or have the same viewpoint.

We realized that it would be extremely interesting and useful to try using the EJ process to retroactively judge an exhibition we had developed and designed together. We've been meaning to do so and are waiting for a window of opportunity in which to do so.

Margie Prager and Jeff Kennedy

The format of our meetings, about two hours long, did not allow us to use the Framework as intended... that is, go by yourself with the form, spend a lot of time reviewing an exhibit, then meet at a later date to discuss. People just don't have that kind of time to commit to it. We did, however, find the Criteria to be useful in framing our discussions as a group.

Stephanie Weaver

Another drawback is that some people may not be comfortable with the level of critical dialogue that takes place. They don't want to participate in conversations that contain as much open criticism as the Framework allows. Our experience shows that the Framework does not become a free-for-all bashing. The Aspects and Criteria are stated positively. The process encourages a balanced approach. In fact, it makes the judges work harder at coming up with positive things to say, even when they've had lots of comments about missed opportunities and counterproductiveness.

I know this. I don't need to do it. But I do need to do it!

Darcie Fohrman

Integrating the Use of the Framework for In-House Exhibition Development

Another question that arose during the development of the Framework was, "Can the Criteria and Aspects be used to develop a new exhibition, not just to rate a completed one?" The answer is yes, and perhaps this use of the Framework has as much potential to positively impact the field as its use for professional development.

The Framework is more than just a list of things to read and post on the wall or throw into a desk drawer. It comes with a compelling process that is built in and ready to use. There are several ways in which this can work for staff members at an institution to develop exhibitions or to improve communication about the exhibit process in general.

Barbara Becker contributed to this chapter.

Visiting Other Exhibitions

When starting a new project, exhibition teams often visit other museums to find out how a subject or collection of artifacts is treated and what design features have been successful. A newly forming project team could use the Framework to assess and discuss one, two, or more exhibitions of their choice.

The in-house team can learn more from their visits as discussions deepen and become more relevant. Since the team members' initial responses, conclusions, and mediating thoughts are written down on the assessment forms, they can be referred to again and again.

Brainstorming an Exhibition

Staffers can use the Framework to guide an initial brainstorm about what they want the exhibition to accomplish. Most exhibit professionals have participated in such sessions. But these brainstorms tend to produce generalizations. Naturally, everyone wants to make the exhibition "engaging" and "meaningful," but what do those terms mean? Do we hear many people stressing that, "Oh, the exhibition must be ergonomically comfortable; its authorship should be clear; or the exhibit ideas must build on themselves"? Perhaps we weren't aware of those issues as critical, or we assumed that others on the team would take care of it later. Turning to the Framework, we find that the Aspects actually define "engaging" and "meaningful," as well as "comfortable" and "reinforcing," in specific, concrete ways. By using the Framework at this initial stage, staffers can create more advocacy on the whole team for Aspects of exhibition excellence. At the very least, team members can master a new and broader vocabulary.

Reviewing and Assessing Plans

Staff members can use the Framework to check exhibition plans midway through the process. The Framework might become a reference with which exhibit developers analyze the white model. This can be a way to assure that the benches the team talked about so many times will actually be specified and ordered; or that the orientation that is really needed at that corner will be noticed again and included.

Aspects as Visitor-Centered Objectives

Visitor-centered objectives are distinct from the exhibition's content goals and objectives, which specify the specific didactic and often unique learning-related objectives. The team could incorporate each Aspect of the more general Framework in its goals for the exhibition as a "visitor-centered experience objective." For example, some of the experience objectives based on the Framework might say

• We will make clear the choices and options of things to do.

> (from Aspect f. of Comfortable: "Choices and options for things to do were clear. Visitors were encouraged to feel in control of their own experiences."); or

• We will make a clear case to the audience of the value of the content as it relates to them.

> (from Aspect b. of Meaningful: "The exhibition made a case that its content has value. The material is timely, important, and resonates with the visitors' values. Meaning is the 'so what.' ")

These visitor-experience objectives would gain equal standing with the content objectives for the project: The visitor-experience objectives would aim at creating an exhibition that is comfortable, engaging, reinforcing, and meaningful, no matter what the specific content. Creating these objectives will also help to bring the visitor-centered principles more thoroughly into team members' awareness. Even a content-centered curator admitted, "The EJ Criteria give content a much better environment."

Dad reads the label; the little girl touches the diorama; the young boy looks at the photograph; Mom keeps an eye on everyone and tries to look at the exhibits, too. Excellent exhibitions afford good experiences under the demanding spectrum of visitors' needs and abilities.

Using the Framework for Formative Evaluation

Formative evaluation of signage or interactives can then proceed with questions derived from the visitor-experience objectives:

- Is an element designed, labeled and placed so that visitors can "get it" and feel confident and motivated to do more?

  (from Aspect b. of Reinforcing: "Challenging or complex exhibit experiences were structured so that visitors who tried to figure them out were likely to say, 'I got it,' and feel confident and motivated to do more.")

- Is it relevant and easily integrated even for those with no prior knowledge or experience?

  (from Aspect a. of Meaningful: "Ideas and objects in the exhibition...were made relevant to and easily integrated into the visitors' experience, regardless of their levels of knowledge or motivation.")

I wasn't kidding about doing this when you're still at the CAD stage as opposed to critiquing it once it's a finished product on the floor and everyone has left and the money is gone. I think this is a really valuable tool in the exhibit development process.

Dan Spock

Maximizing Summative Evaluation

Once an exhibition is open, doing a summative evaluation to find out how the audience responded and what they learned is critical for the institution and exhibit team members. You are eager to know, What did we do right? Carried out at the same time, an in-house Excellent Judges assessment can help to deepen understanding of the strengths and weaknesses of the completed exhibition.

A new panel of judges made up of peers who have not been part of the exhibit team could also carry out an EJ assessment. Exhibit team members can be "flies on the wall" during the discussion, thus getting more professional feedback on the exhibition.

I didn't want the EJ group to visit the Conservatory after we opened only to shake their heads in despair and wonder what we were thinking when we made that decision. So, before things were final, we asked our group to evaluate a set of exhibits and give us their feedback. We did this last week and it was very helpful. We've rewritten labels in response to specific suggestions and are reviewing the whole show to incorporate some suggestions throughout.

Kitty Connolly

Applying some of the Framework vocabulary to the discussion of the visitor-feedback evaluation will help the team to communicate more effectively about how to make use of the evaluation study's results. The EJ discussions can help to interpret a trend observed in the evaluation data and will help the institution be aware of that issue for the next exhibition.

Using the Framework to Teach Museum Studies

Eugene Dillenburg contributed to this section.

The Framework was developed for use by professionals, but it is also appropriate for museum studies students, who are interested but have not yet entered the profession. In the summer of 2002, Eugene Dillenburg (one of the original Excellent Judges in Chicago) taught an undergraduate course to 16 students in the Museum Studies Program at Michigan State University in East Lansing. Entitled "Assessing Excellence in Public Education Exhibitions," the course was designed around an early version of the Framework–using it as a means for looking at and thinking critically about exhibitions. Based on this experience, this section discusses what to expect when using the Framework with museum studies students.

A Solid Foundation

As a distillation of current knowledge about what makes exhibitions work, the Framework is singularly powerful. Many definitions of exhibit excellence originated with individual professionals, and thus tend to be personal and idiosyncratic. The Framework, on the other hand, is firmly based on decades of research about education and visitor behavior. To walk a museum studies class through the Rationale for each Criterion and Aspect is to provide a mini-course in contemporary exhibit theory.

Learning the Language

Working with real exhibitions turns theory into something concrete. The Framework provides a language for applying experience from a visitor-centered perspective. But students don't have the professional experience to understand all the words at first. Even something as basic as what constitutes "an exhibition" can prove elusive. In the first test run, when students were asked to review one exhibition in a local museum, they came back with comments about the bathrooms, parking, and admissions procedures, and one person included comments about another exhibition. Recognizing the boundaries of an exhibition–where it begins and ends, what's included, what's not–can be difficult for the uninitiated, including visitors. The purview of the Framework is one exhibition at a time.

Another question that always comes up with professionals whenever we've introduced the tool is the issue of identity. What perspective shall we use? The content expert, exhibit professional, the "typical" visitor–whatever that may be? Not surprisingly, the students had the same question. The Excellent Judges struggled mightily with this issue, and an entire chapter of this book is devoted to how we eventually resolved it. (See "Taking a Visitor-Centered Perspective" on page 25.)

Differences Between Using the Framework With Students and Professionals

A typical judging session involves a half-dozen or so professionals. In the class, there might be more. Dillenburg's class had 16 students. It was difficult to facilitate a discussion with so many people and make sure they all had their say before class ended for the day.

Typically judges view one exhibition, on their own, at a time of their own choosing, and they might have several days to reflect before meeting for the discussion. A second exhibition may not be viewed for a month or more. With the compressed schedule of a university course, students might be judging more exhibitions in a matter of a few weeks. If field trips are involved, students usually go in a group and often discuss exhibitions immediately after each is visited.

On a field trip to Chicago, Dillenburg's class met with several museum professionals and discussed their work. This is a deviation from the tool's protocol, which scrupulously avoids getting the insider's story on the creators' intentions from any place other than the exhibition itself. But the professional development needs of students were such that it was important to expose them to multiple perspectives for the benefit of the class, not just using the Framework.

Looking Beyond the Obvious

Exhibit professionals are trained to consider how diverse audiences will view our work. We discuss ways to be inclusive and welcoming, taking into consideration the psychological comfort that visitors will experience in exhibitions. One of the Aspects of the Comfortable Criterion is attribution: "Authorship, biases, intent, and perspectives of the exhibition were revealed, identified, or attributed. The exhibits reveal who is talking, fact from fiction or opinion, the real from the not real." Students have not yet had these debates. Once it has been pointed out, however, they quickly learn to be sensitive to this issue, and it generated some of the liveliest discussions.

An example: In *Chocolate* at the Field Museum, one section described the role of slavery in the early chocolate trade. Some students wondered what such a heavy topic was doing in this otherwise frothy show; another felt it was "aggressively PC." Others thought the subject was handled very evenhandedly, and some noted the dramatic contrast between the elegance of European chocolate drinkers and the slaves who harvested the beans. These sorts of issues exist in many exhibitions but had been overlooked in earlier exhibit discussions with the students.

The related Aspect of attribution came up toward the end of the *Chocolate* galleries. A display on the modern chocolate industry presented the stories of various people involved in growing, manufacturing, and distribution. While some students liked the human touch, the uniformly smiling faces struck others as false.

The class later learned from their discussion with the exhibit developers that these were in fact pictures of actors–not farmers and workers–taken from a stock photo book. The students were aghast. They felt they had been lied to. This became a touchstone for the rest of the course. Again and again, students questioned whether they could believe an exhibition or whether it was lying to them. One even went so far as to question artifact ID labels: "How do I know this is really an 18th-century French goblet?"

In the final museum studies class meeting, several students noted that they had gained confidence in their judgments through experience, and they felt that their later scores were more accurate and more soundly reasoned than their early ones. Their ratings also showed more uniformity. Having a group work through several rounds of using the Framework moved the judges–students in this case–up the learning curve.

Similarities among Students and Museum Professionals

In many respects, student's reflections on the mechanics of the tool were very similar to those of professionals. Both groups debated whether the tool should be more of an objective "checklist" of specific features or, given the variety of exhibitions out there, perhaps it should remain open-ended and thus more subjective. The students also raised the same questions as the pros did about whether it is possible to truly take a visitor's perspective. And, like the pros, the students found great value in making Call-Outs and discussing their impressions.

The students reported the same benefits that professionals often note. They felt the tool had helped them a great deal, compelling them to look closely at exhibitions and to think critically about their gallery experience. The students also liked the process of giving numerical scores. Again, it made them think critically, reaching conclusions based on their observations, then staking a position and defending it. They acknowledged that the discussions afterwards, hearing what others had to say, were the most valuable part of the exercise. They saw the tool not as an end in itself, but as a catalyst for understanding and improvement. Again, this is precisely what professionals cite as the greatest benefit of the tool.

It has been my experience that bringing our entire institution around to a place where we all agree that the visitor is at the center of our work has indeed been a long process. Maybe things have changed and all the new professionals coming into the field understand this already.

Colleen Blair

Improving the Museum Studies Course

Despite being developed for and by museum professionals, the tool worked well in helping students look at and think about exhibits in a critical fashion. Plans are underway to develop another MSU class using the tool, building on the experience with the first group. For instance, the professors hope to include more exhibit theory so the students understand that the EJ Criteria and Aspects weren't pulled at random but rather reflect the accumulated knowledge of the field. Since discussion rather than scoring has emerged as the most valuable part of the process, students will probably spend more time talking about fewer exhibitions. This may require restructuring the class to create smaller discussion groups. One significant challenge will be providing more time for reflection between viewing the exhibit and holding the discussion. Given that the course runs during an 8-week semester, and the field trip to Chicago will take three or four days, this may not be possible.

Perhaps the greatest challenge of all is how to balance the students' very reasonable desire to discuss exhibitions with museum professionals against the Framework's strict focus on the experience of visitors.

In our last meeting, one student asked if knowing the Framework would help her get a job. If she mentioned it at an interview, would they know what she was talking about?

Eugene Dillenburg

Using the Framework
with Art Museums

Eugene Dillenburg,
Lynn LaBate, and
Mary Beth Trautwein
contributed to this
chapter.

The Excellent Judges project focused primarily on the needs of science museums. As the tool evolved, we realized that our Criteria addressed issues of universal importance and were, in fact, relevant to all types of museums. Most of the exhibitions we visited and used in our process were in some way related to science, but their settings were diverse: a natural history museum, a planetarium, a zoo, an aquarium, a science museum, and a children's museum.

In workshops we presented early versions of the Framework as having applicability for all topics. Our assumption was that art exhibitions can be interpretive using the same modalities that other types of museums use, and their designs and aesthetics are part of the exhibit environment and visitor experience. Not everyone agreed. During a question-and-answer session after presenting the Framework concepts at the Getty Museum in November 2002, one participant said the tool was not relevant to her work, as it didn't specifically address aesthetics. What did she mean?

Maybe she defined aesthetics to mean art exhibitions that do not include interpretive messages or shows without didactic intent. Art curators often mount exhibitions that include an introductory text panel and "tombstone" labels (with the artist's name, medium, dates, donor, accession number and other identifications), maybe a video, few if any other graphic or text panels, and no interactive elements. If this was the kind of aesthetic display she was referring to, yes, we agree, the Framework is less useful. But that would be true for any minimally or underinterpreted exhibit topic or display (e.g., a botanic garden that's just about looking at plants, or a children's museum area that is just about focused play). If there is a low diversity of formats (e.g., graphics, text, audiovisuals, models, phenomena) or sensual modalities (other than sight), Framework users would have fewer specific elements to discuss, but they'd still be able to talk about their overall experiences.

Certainly, art curators expend tremendous care in choosing the objects, grouping them into rooms, selecting wall colors, and installing the pieces in a particular sequence, all of which affect how they are perceived. The way the exhibit is designed, the way the art is selected, and the image the museum projects—all these reflect the aesthetics of the objects and institution. The goal of the interpretive materials—whichever ones are present—is to enhance looking at the art.

On one hand, interpretive materials reflect or respond to the aesthetics of the art objects, while on the other, they are part of the aesthetics in the whole environment. Some art museum practitioners argue that interpretive labels interfere with the aesthetic experience; others argue that the benefits of interpretive materials for the majority of visitors outweigh any interference with aesthetics, especially when diverse audiences are targeted. The Framework does not take a position for or against labels; it asks whether an experience with features that are known to help visitors receive and understand interpretation has been made possible: Did visitors feel in control of their own experience? Were social interactions promoted? Did visitors feel competent? Was the "so what?" of the exhibition apparent?

An art exhibition (or other topic) could be highly interpretive and have an abundance of evidence for many of the Criteria and Aspects of the Framework

I asked myself how hard will it be for Mr. and Mrs. Visitor to feel competent in my art museum. Are the exhibits there just to demonstrate our expertise? Where does it leave our visitors if that's the case?

Getty Workshop participant

without using any interpretive content or devices. But if there are none, and the logic behind the installation is not transparent to an art-novice visitor, the exhibition cannot be said to be excellent from a visitor-centered perspective.

To test these assumptions, to see if the tool really does work with exhibits that interpret aesthetics, we asked our Getty colleagues to use the Framework with one of their installations. They chose to assess *Statue of an Emperor: A Conservation Partnership*. It contained one large object, supporting text, graphics, and video. They had no trouble applying the Criteria of comfort, engagement, reinforcement, and meaningfulness to it. They also gave us feedback on the layout: they wanted more space for writing Call-outs and Rationales.

It took a couple times reading the protocol and referring to the Web site to feel more comfortable with the terms. After completing it, I felt, overall, this was a great tool for turning subjective feelings into a useful rating system. It has me thinking more freshly about exhibits and their ability to connect with a visitor.

Mary Beth Trautwein

If subject matter is merely displayed in and of itself with no suggestion of a larger context, no encouragement to make personal connections, or no avenue for engaging in discussion, then the primary thrust of the exhibition is not interpretive. In such cases, too much responsibility is placed on the visitor to do all of the work without assistance, limiting the chance of a change taking place.

Matt Sikora

According to the art museum educators, "Aesthetics are an unspoken element in every aspect of art museum exhibitions and collections." Indeed aesthetics, as realized through exhibit design, are vitally important to the meaning of any exhibit, whether art, science, or history. No definition of excellence can possibly overlook this crucial facet. The Framework focuses on the experience in the gallery. To the extent that aesthetics influence that experience–and the influence is great and undeniable–then they are indeed embraced by the Framework.

Art museum exhibitions using interpretive elements, including extended labels, graphics, and video, also can be assessed with the Framework.

PART IV

THEORETICAL UNDERPINNINGS

Part IV discusses the assumptions, theories, and research that underlie the Framework. We take a practitioner's approach, not an academic one, but we value both. The references cited and the empirical practices leading us to these conclusions come from a variety of sources, mostly within the museum community. Publications such as *Curator, NAME Exhibitionist,* and *Visitor Studies* will be familiar to many readers.

Comparing the Framework to Other Methods of Reviewing Exhibitions

In developing the Framework we were informed and inspired by other sources of review and criticism in the museum field, such as the American Association of Museums' *Standards for Museum Exhibitions*, the critiquing sessions at the AAM annual meetings, NAME *Exhibitionist* newsletter discussions, other articles, and countless exhibition evaluations, primarily summative studies. In this chapter, we will discuss what distinguishes the Framework from other methods of reviewing exhibitions.

The first and biggest difference between using the Framework and using other forms of review is that with the Framework there is usually no product (e.g., a report, article, award, summary) to distribute or share. Evaluations result in reports; critiques and reviews are often published in museum journals, and the AAM award is announced at the annual conference where the winning entry receives a plaque. With the Framework, the "product" is the process: The people who benefit from the Framework are the people who share the experience of using it to review an exhibition.

There are further differences and distinctions between the purpose, process and products of the Framework and other forms of review, as well as some similarities.

What standards do I apply? My standards. I'm comparing the exhibit I'm critiquing against the perfect exhibit that only exists in my mind.

Don Hughes

Comparison of six methods of reviewing museum exhibitions that are completed and open to the public.

Method	Conducted By	Question Asked
Summative Evaluation	Evaluators: in-house or consultants	Did it work?
Exhibition Critiques	Individuals	Did I like it?
Reviews	Individuals	What's it about?
AAM Standards	Members of AAM SPCs	How does it measure up to the standards?
Critical Appraisal	Visitor studies experts	Where are the problems?
Excellent Judges Framework	Museum practitioners	Where and why do we agree or disagree?

Primary Purpose	Product	Primary Audience
Accountability to funders; measure of objectives achieved	Report	Institution, exhibit developers
Share opinions	Speech or article	Profession
Public relations	Publication	Readers, visitors
Present annual award	Award	Profession, institution
Aid remedial fixes before summative evaluation	Report	Institution, exhibit developers
Discussion for professional development	The process	Participants

Summative Evaluations

Summative evaluations of exhibitions rely on systematically collected feedback from visitors. Standard practices of evaluation, such as interviews, surveys, and trackings, are well known and learnable (i.e., they are not personal or idiosyncratic). Summative evaluation is often (although certainly not always) goal related; that is, evaluation looks for evidence that the exhibition's objectives were met and defines success in those terms. The question exhibit evaluators ask is, "Did it work?" or "Was it effective?" Evaluation usually compares visitor feedback about the exhibition to the exhibit developer's intentions and objectives. Harris Shettel says that the main basis for saying a museum exhibition is "good" is to find out what the exhibition was supposed to do and then to see whether it did (Shettel 1994).

Summative evaluations are carried out by trained evaluators, often consultants for hire, for museums that are obligated by a funding agency or operating on their own volition to find out what the impact of an exhibition was on their audiences.

The Framework is not a replacement for other forms of judging excellence or effectiveness that use direct forms of feedback from visitors. It's not a substitute for doing visitor studies. The degree to which an Excellent Judges review agrees with or differs from a summative evaluation of the same exhibition is an outstanding research question at this time; early indications are that they converge. (See the *Wild Reef* case study on pages 133 to 137.)

Critiques

Critiques are the opinions of informed professionals, given their training, experience, and personal biases. The critic asks, "Did I like it, and why or why not?" Critiques are not intended to be objective. Depending on the critic, his or her opinions may be informed by and compared with a broad range of knowledge of the field. Criticism is analysis and consists of value judgments measured against the "doctrinal allegiance" of the critic (Chambers 1999). The critic applies his or her own standards, the ones that exist in his or her mind. It's up to the listener to judge the value of the critic's opinion.

A critique of an exhibition is usually carried out by an individual, with or without permission or invitation by the museum being critiqued. The exhibition's intent may or may not play a strong role in the critique, and the intent might be interpreted differently by the critic than by the hosting institution.

Probably the most well-known and public exhibition critiques were the AAM sessions at the annual conventions, from 1990 to 2000–the decade during which they were organized by Kathy McLean. The sessions were always well-attended, and the audio tapes of them were bestsellers after the meetings. One of the aspects that made them popular was the critics' frankness in their less-than-positive impressions. Discussions following these sessions were often long and loud and led to some provoking publications that contrasted the issues of criticism, standards, and the AAM exhibition awards (Serrell 1993; Spillman 1993).

The Framework is similar to critiques in that the review process includes consideration of negative reflections and delineation of missed opportunities. It therefore has the potential to also be threatening in its judgments. The Framework, however, helps the assessors move to a broader range of considerations and a shared set of values.

I've given enough critiques to know I often piss people off. I probably offend more folks than I endear. I don't set out to make people unhappy. I want the exhibit I'm going to review to be good. Critiques are a good way to start conversations about the art and craft of presenting exhibits, and we need as many ways as possible to have these conversations.

Don Hughes

Reviews

Reviews vary widely. Depending on the author, reviews of exhibitions may sound more objective or subjective. The reviewer's intent is often not clearly stated, and his or her qualifications may not include museum practice in visitor studies, exhibition development, or scholarship in the subject matter. The intentions of the exhibit developers are often a main focus. In a guide for writing reviews, Phyllis Rabineau includes the suggestion to phone the people most directly responsible for the exhibition and ask them questions about their agendas, intentions, and constraints (Rabineau 1994).

In a review of reviews, Paulette McManus points out that they typically contain excessive praise, ignore or lightly skim over exhibition faults, ignore accountability to claimed communication goals, and employ descriptive rather than analytical methods, and, therefore, fail to offer information that can be helpful for improving museum practices (McManus 1986).

In developing the Framework, we wanted to be clear about its purpose and who we were, to include the

---

Perhaps we could devise a system of reporting so that all the judgments are assessed in the same way. This draws a nice distinction with "critique," in which an individual reviewer is given free rein to be as subjective as he wants. I could theoretically critique an exhibit based solely on its label text, paying no attention whatever to design, lighting, collections, orientation, etc. As a judge, I would be required to look at all those areas. I am still free to be responsibly subjective within those areas, drawing upon my personal experience.

Eugene Dillenburg

---

consideration of both positive and negative Aspects, to base the Criteria on practical research findings, and to assist museum professionals in doing a better job. While the Excellent Judges are not without individual bias, the Framework offers a more focused and structured alternative to critiques or reviews.

Are there standards for film criticism? No. Only personal opinions. Any possible list of standards is an inspiration to the exceptions it suggests.

Roger Ebert

The AAM Standards for Museum Exhibitions and Indicators of Excellence

In 1997 three standing professional committees (SPCs) of the American Association of Museums (CARE, NAME, and CurCom, with help and input from other SPCs) developed standards to be used as guidelines for judging the entries in the annual exhibition competition. Museums that competed for the award submitted application forms and other materials (e.g., label text, photographs of displays, walk-through videos) to three judges, each a representative of one committee, who discussed their choices and picked the winner(s) jointly at a meeting. When using the AAM guidelines to assess an exhibition, the judges ask, "Did it achieve or exceed the Standards?"

The AAM Standards include many important exhibit concerns that are not obvious or available during a normal, unguided, public experience of going to the exhibition. These issues include the exhibition's budget, conservation and mounting techniques, security measures, special educational programming, or the process of the exhibition's creation. The perspective of the AAM's criteria is mainly on presentation and intent. The standards are listed in six categories (Audience Awareness, Content, Collections, Interpretation and Communication, Design and Production, and Ergonomics), each of which is followed by a question. Following the question, there are specific ways the category might be expressed that would constitute effectiveness for that category. For example:

Audience Awareness

Did the audience respond well to the exhibiton, and was the response consistent with the exhibition's goals?

- Decisions about content, means of expression, and design are based on decisions about the intended audience.

- Visitors are given information in a variety of formats to accommodate various needs and preferences. If not, why not?

Content

Does the exhibition respect the integrity of its content?

- Significant ideas, based on appropriate authority, are clearly expressed through reference to objects in the exhibition.
- The content reflects current knowledge of the subject.
- There is a sufficient number of objects to present the subject of the exhibition.

Collections

Have conservation and security matters been appropriately addressed?

- Objects are mounted appropriately.
- The requirements of good conservation (light levels, climate control) and security are met.

When the Chicago EJs first reviewed the AAM's Standards, we concluded that we did not have the expertise to assess many of these issues. Most of us would simply not be able to tell if an exhibition showed evidence for achieving standards about security, climate control requirements, mounting techniques, and whether or not the content was current, significant, or accurate. Nor could we tell how the decisions were made about the content and intended audience, production techniques, marketing strategies, or mission statements. All that would require obtaining lots of insider information from the museum that developed the exhibition. These are all important and interesting factors to think about when judging an exhibition, but many of them did not deal with the essence of experience and clarity we were looking for.

The AAM Standards have another section called "Indicators of Excellence in Museum Exhibitions."

Why didn't we use them? Because these "indicators" had to do with content and were hard to define. For example, "Indicators" included:

• An aspect of the exhibition is innovative.

• The exhibition presents new information.

• The exhibition synthesizes and presents existing knowledge and/or collection materials in a provocative way.

We wanted to create a set of standards that could be applied solely by looking at and experiencing the exhibition without behind-the-scenes details. We cut out all categories, requirements, and specification that were not visible or knowable from a visitor's viewpoint. We brought in all of the ways that a museum exhibition is organized and presents itself to the user.

Nevertheless, among the AAM's Standards and the EJ Framework, there are some strong parallel and equivalent concerns. For example:

AAM–Audience Awareness

• Visitors are given information in a variety of formats to accommodate various needs and preferences. If not, why not?

> Equivalent to EJ Framework
> Criterion of Engaging, Aspect e.

• The exhibition is designed to accommodate those who wish to skim as well as those who wish to take more time. If not, why not?

> Equivalent to EJ Framework
> Criterion of Engagement, Aspect f. and
> Criterion of Reinforcing, Aspect a.

AAM–Interpretation/Communication

• There is a discernible pattern to the way content is presented, and if not, there is a good reason why not.

> Equivalent to EJ Framework
> Criterion of Reinforcing, Aspect c.

- Assumptions and points-of-view are clearly identified. If appropriate to the subject matter, the exhibition need not provide definitive answers. Raising questions and providing a forum for ideas may suffice.

> Equivalent to EJ Framework
> Criterion of Comfortable, Aspect g.

AAM–Ergonomics

- There is seating, as appropriate.

> Equivalent to EJ Framework
> Criterion of Comfortable, Aspect b.

The AAM's Standards separate "Design" from "Interpretation." The EJ Framework does not. Instead, the Framework expects that the exhibition design supports the interpretation to effectively communicate the ideas. We concur with Leinhardt and Knutson's conclusion, "When the designed environment functions in support of the message of the exhibition as intended, it seamlessly blends into the experience" (Leinhardt and Knutson 2004).

One of the biggest ways the process of AAM's judging differs from that of the Framework is that the Excellent Judges visit the actual exhibition and experience it firsthand. The AAM judges look at photographs and video and read narratives and label copy. It is logistically and financially unfeasible to send the AAM

The AAM Standards are available on line

This document is available on the internet at
www.n-a-m-e.org/standards.html.

Readers are encouraged to visit the Web site to find an updated version of the AAM Standards when they become available.

judges around the country to visit all of the entries each year. Also, temporary shows are included in the yearly competition, and awards are given for exhibitions that have been de-installed or may come down a short time later.

The Framework is not used to give awards or to reach consensus about the best or the worst exhibitions. The Excellent Judges ask each other, "Where and why do we agree and disagree on our assessments?" Yet, after a group of the same EJs has conducted several discussions and rating exercises together, they will have some fairly strong ideas and evidence about which of those exhibitions showed more excellent Aspects than others.

A critique is the act of an individual. It's a pastime that many of us do privately, but few do publicly. Thus, criticism may seem a bit antisocial when it's shared. It makes us nervous.

Don Hughes

All of these types of reviews can ultimately help the institutions, the practitioners, the profession as a whole, and the visitor, by spurring us on to create better exhibits. But part of what differentiates the types is who is the primary intended audience for a given review.

Eugene Dillenburg

102

Critical Appraisal

Critical appraisal is a review done by someone well-versed in visitor studies literature. Its main purpose is to identify obvious and potential problems in a new exhibition before conducting a summative evaluation (Bitgood and Benefield 1995). While there are several differences between critical appraisal and the Framework as to the purpose, the product, and the audience, the visitor studies expert who conducts a critical appraisal would see many similarities between the Framework's Criteria and the appraiser's concerns for improving the visitor experience. Visitor studies inform both processes.

The critical appraisal looks for exhibit weaknesses that can be easily fixed before collecting data on visitors' responses to the exhibition. "The client has at the completion of the study an itemized list of those things in the exhibition that should be corrected to improve visitor response..." (Shettel 1994). For example, recommendations regarding problems relating to orientation, lighting levels, label placement, wording in texts, or sightlines might be the outcome of a critical appraisal. Critical appraisal can also be used to review older exhibitions before undertaking major renovations. Questions asked by an appraiser are usually related to achieving the exhibit's teaching objectives, and findings from research and evaluation are used to predict impact.

Roger Miles, formerly the head of the department of public services at the British Museum of Natural History in London, writes:

> Critical appraisal is a mixed blessing. It provides a subjective judgment that is only as good as the critic.... On the other hand, critical appraisal works; it is possible to get useful advice on how to improve the exhibition, and in the absence of more objective guidance, this knowledge is worth having (Miles 1988).

Harris Shettel and Steven Bitgood have taught workshops on critical appraisal at the Visitor Studies

Association's conferences for many years, but there are no published references on how to conduct one. To obtain their checklist you have to take the workshop or borrow it from someone who has.

The critical appraisal checklist includes 26 questions about orientation, circulation, label text, and factors within and between exhibits. Certainly all of these factors are important to creating clear, accessible, understandable exhibits. Many of the items on the checklist address concerns of concept, message, and comprehensibility, and label length, legibility, and content. For example:

☐ Is there a label telling what the exhibition is all about?

☐ Is the label placed in a location where it will be read?

☐ Are the letter sizes adequate?

☐ Are the text labels short (50-75 words)?

☐ Can labels be easily understood?

☐ Can the message be communicated in a brief period of time?

☐ Is it clear how the exhibit displays are organized?

Overall, critical appraisal looks for problems and ways to solve them. If this is the kind of exhibit study that a client needs, and it needs to be done quickly, it's a good choice. Alternatively, the Framework takes a more positive approach, looking for indicators of excellence and rating them according to some general criteria. Missed opportunities would certainly get noted as well at the level of specificity that the critical appraisal checklist provides. "Perhaps the most difficult aspect of a critical appraisal is minimizing personal bias and restricting the appraisal to empirical findings," say Bitgood and Benefield, and those challenges exist for the Framework, too.

The Framework's Aspects cover the same issues and concerns as the critical appraisal checklist and many others as well. Here are the EJ ones that echo some of the critical appraisal examples above; the EJ Aspects are more comprehensive and less prescriptive:

Comfortable a.
> Physical and conceptual orientation devices were present.

Comfortable e.
> There was a good ergonomic fit. Exhibit elements could be read, viewed, and used with ease.

Comfortable f.
> Choices and options for things to do were clear. Visitors were encouraged to feel in control of their own experiences.

Reinforcing b.
> Challenging or complex exhibit experiences were structured so that visitors who tried to figure them out were likely to say, "I got it," and feel confident and motivated to do more.

Reinforcing c.
> The presentation had a logic. It held together intellectually in a way that was easily followed and understood.

Contracting with a group of Excellent Judges could provide an interesting expansion on the idea of a critical appraisal–with several added benefits: There is more than one person's opinion; the Framework provides a more comprehensive view of the visitor experience; and the protocol can embrace stakeholders in the process.

A final note about comparisons among critical appraisal, the AAM Standards, and the Framework. We strove to be guiding with our four Criteria and 23 Aspects, but not prescriptive. The Framework identifies the important Aspects of an excellent exhibition, but it does not tell you how to achieve them; that is up to the individual exhibition makers. Critical appraisal is more prescriptive with its 26-item checklist and is heavily focused on text/label issues. The AAM Standards are less prescriptive, but still are fairly directive in the 29 ways to achieve or demonstrate their six categories. For example, compare all three with how each deals with orientation:

Critical Appraisal: Is there a label telling what the exhibition is all about?

AAM Standards: Orientation at the start and throughout the exhibition provides visitors with a conceptual, physical, and affective overview of the exhibition.

EJ Framework: Physical and conceptual orientation devices were present.

An exhibition developer's time would be well spent becoming familiar with all of these methods of assessing exhibitions. The Framework, we think, is the most accessible for all practitioners.

The Framework does not count visitor attendance, note demographic categories, or survey visitor satisfaction. For those data, other visitor studies are necessary.

FAQ: What won't the Framework tell you about your exhibition?

The Framework will not tell you how many visitors came to the exhibition or what their demographic and psychographic characteristics (motivations, expectations) were. It will not tell you what visitors liked or what they learned. It will not tell you what visitors did in the exhibition, how much time they spent, where they stopped, or where they interacted socially. For these qualities and measurements, you must conduct a visitor study. The Framework can only tell you how a group of professionals rated the exhibition against preexisting visitor-centered standards for excellence in interpretive exhibitions, but that is useful knowledge.

The Framework should not be used as a substitute where evaluation of actual visitor feedback had been promised to funders. The Framework is a great complement to doing visitor studies, but it is not a substitute. Using the Framework is, however, better than doing nothing to assess the quality of the exhibition. It is cheaper than hiring an evaluation consultant to do a study, and the results will be very useful to the exhibit developers, especially if they are involved in the process. But if the stakeholders were promised a summative evaluation, that's what they should get.

FAQ: Does the Framework tell an institution whether the exhibition meets its communication goals?

It doesn't. Other tools such as visitor studies are better for measuring how well the intent of the museum was carried out. This Framework looks at what is provided on the floor and whether an exhibition works from that point of view. Evidence of excellence, according to the Framework, would include multiple good examples of opportunities for interesting, clear, sensory, relevant, meaningful, engaging, valuable, reinforcing, transcendent experiences–which may or may not align with the exhibit's intended communication goals. But chances are, if all those aforementioned experiences were actually possible for the majority of the audience in an exhibition, the exhibition was probably planned and executed with clear and accessible communication goals.

FAQ: To get a visitor perspective, why not just interview visitors?

Visitor studies are irreplaceable for getting certain types of information, but the Framework process can help describe some features of an exhibition that are difficult to track by observing or interviewing visitors. Visitors don't know the language for describing exhibits (they say things such as "I just like it"), and few have enough sophistication about an exhibition's possibilities to provide a full critique. In particular, visitors seldom address the question, "What's missing?" although they certainly are aware of broken, confusing, or uncomfortable exhibit elements. The process of using the Framework requires some familiarity with visitor studies, informal education, education theory, exhibit planning and design, interpretive strategies, exhibit evaluation, cognitive psychology, and other related fields. The more the better. We don't expect visitors to have this background in theory or practice. The Framework helps define the industry's best practices, and it is used by professionals who are acquainted with them.

Furthermore, the EJ process takes a commitment of hours for discussion, not something that would be reasonable to ask of visitors without making appointments and paying them, like a focus group. A completely reworded, different framework could be created to get at many of the same issues in a nonprofessional language, but that would be a whole other project.

It's not the visitor's job to tell you how to make better exhibitions: It's the museum practitioner's responsibility to seek professional development—to share knowledge, to challenge ideas, and to foster creativity.

FAQ: Does the Framework address truth, accuracy, and good scholarship?

The Framework is not a tool for judging scholarship, but rather for judging experience. Visitors don't know whether the most up-to-date scientific theories are included, so other evaluation techniques must be used to determine this. One Aspect of the Comfortable Criterion, however, is making authorship and attribution clear to visitors. This comes into play where visitors may feel some level of discomfort about content. One example is making sponsors apparent when there is a potential conflict of interest, such as a gas company sponsoring an exhibit about petroleum.

Could a socially unacceptable/unethical exhibition be judged to be excellent? This seems possible, but it's unlikely because issues of pluralism, authority, voice, attribution, and accountability that the Framework raises would need to be addressed adequately to be judged excellent in terms of comfort.

Matt Sikora

Research and Other Studies
Inform the Framework's Criteria

Barbara Becker contributed to this section.

The development of the Framework for Assessing Excellence in Exhibitions from a Visitor-centered Perspective proceeded on the premise that certain core conditions in exhibitions will heighten the *opportunity* for learning to take place. This chapter provides citations of research, theory, practice, and opinion from a variety of disciplines supporting the links between the four Criteria and the process of personal learning.

I think it would be useful for a lot of people to know how you've arrived at these particular categories. These aren't things that are just your opinion, what you think are important. There's really a whole body of research that shows just how important these characteristics are in an exhibition to make learning happen.

Dan Spock

Museum exhibitions are almost universally seen as places where informal learning takes place. Museums obtain public and private funding on the premise that they are reaching hundreds of thousands of people yearly with their educational messages. Yet learning as a result of exhibitions has been an extremely challenging process to study and has not been demonstrated in such a way as to produce generalizations about cause and effect.

We defined "learning" inclusively to reflect ongoing discussions in the literature about what in fact constitutes learning in informal settings (Falk and Dierking 1992, 1995). The definition below was adapted from Serrell (1996), and we feel it reflects the broadest aspects of learning: didactic, affective and experiential, as well as meaning-making:

Learning in museums is a change, small or large, that happens in a person's cognitive structure as a result of a new integration–new information, attitudes, feelings, or skills; new connections between prior knowledge and new information, and/or a new reflection of something already known.

Following is a survey of professional literature that provides the foundation for our Framework's four Criteria: Comfortable, Engaging, Reinforcing, and Meaningful. With the help of professional resources (Museum Learning Collaborative's annotated literature on their Web site) and colleagues (Chandler Screven), we gathered evidence for direct and indirect relationships between each of the Criteria and learning from the literature on museum studies, behavioral and cognitive psychology, environmental psychology, human factors analysis, and other sources.

It was not always possible to provide one-on-one verification for each of the Aspects of the Criteria because there are multiple and overlapping sources. An article may be more suggestive than specific, or a specific study may apply to more than one Aspect. Referring to the Framework on pages 41 to 46 of this book will help you recognize the specific relationships.

Good orientation affords physical and psychological comfort: Knowing how big the exhibition is, what it contains, and what it's about helps learners be receptive to new experiences.

Rather than being an exhaustive and complete review of the literature, it is a compilation of the most relevant resources–some of our most-used favorites.

Literature Related to Issues of Comfort

Comfort may be the most well-documented factor in creating the opportunity for learning. Hood (1993) established the importance of comfort, and a sense of being cared about, for the purpose of drawing people to visit museums, which is an indisputable first step to learning in exhibits. Balling and Falk (1980) demonstrated that an environment that is too novel for certain individuals can actually impede learning by producing anxiety rather than comfort.

Csikszentmihalyi and Hermanson (1995b), Evans (1995), and Hedge (1995) discuss ways in which inadequate seating or resting places, loud or overly bright or dark spaces, and disorderly (unclear or cluttered) "information design" can lead to anxiety, which interferes with learning. These are defined as elements of "the physical environment shown to influence various psychological processes that, in turn, are assumed to affect learning" (Evans 1995).

The need for "advance organizers" (orientation) and wayfinding prior to and throughout exhibition viewing is also well-documented. When people know what to expect and can make informed choices about what they can do, they will be more likely to learn. (See Crane, Nicholson, Chen, and Bitgood 1994; also Griggs 1983; Kintsch 1994; Ausubel 1960, 1968; Wolf 1992; Zueck 1988.) Conceptual orientation presented by a guide or in a film seemed to be more effective than signage (Hayward and Brydon-Miller 1984).

Evidence that label tone, or "voice," affects learning is cited by McManus (1989). Ogbu (1995) provides discussion and resources on the role of cultural differences on learning. Others discuss a "participatory" model of learning, in which museums and visitors become "a community of learners making individual and shared contributions to understanding" (Matusov and Rogoff 1995, p 101; also see Falk and Dierking 1992). See the chapter on pages 78 to 83 about using the Framework with students: It shows examples of how the attribution of information can have an impact on a visitor's experience.

Exhibitions with controversial or even repulsive topics can still be comfortable if visitors are given opportunities to understand and appreciate that the exhibition's content has value. Exhibitions with uncomfortable content will need to closely attend to strengthening other factors–such as engagement (without overwhelming), meaningfulness, accessibility, inspiration, or even humor. "Visitors also seem prepared to take on controversial content, not just controversy over content" (Leinhardt and Knutson 2004).

Discomfort in the form of "cognitive dissonance" (content or design that creates contradictions) is not a negative Aspect to an exhibition experience (Semper 1990), so long as it is not too prolonged, unresolved, or intense to the point of preventing other experiences. Exhibit developers might want to sample some cognitive dissonance themselves by reviewing the amount of time visitors actually spend in exhibitions (Serrell 1998) compared to their museum's expectations, assumptions, or desires.

References about Engaging Experiences in Exhibitions

Without engagement there is no learning. There is considerable evidence that exhibitions that are engaging, exhibitions that draw visitors in and keep their attention (by being "fun," interactive, responsive, restorative, etc.), can lead to learning (Bitgood, Patterson, and Benefield 1988; Borun and Flexer 1984; Csikszentmihalyi and Hermanson 1995a,b; Evans 1995; Griggs 1990; Harvey 1995; Horn 1998; Koran, et al 1984; Malone 1981; Miles 1986; Screven 1973, 1974, 1975). Bitgood established that immersion environments encourage visitors to spend more time and therefore be more likely to remember things about the subject (Bitgood 1990b).

An engaging exhibition (or any other engaging task) is one that will encourage people to spend more time, which has been well-documented to be a first step to learning (Serrell 1998; Shettel 1995; Peart 1984; Koran, Foster, and Koran 1989; Crane, Nicholson, Chen, and Bitgood 1994; Bransford 1993; Gagne 1985). "Time spent at the exhibit turned out to be directly related to Learning Level; families with higher-level scores spent significantly more time at the exhibits" (Borun et al. 1998).

Studies by Silverman (1990) and especially Borun (1996, 1997) have established the key importance of social learning in museums. Leinhardt and Knutson documented the essential role of conversation between visitors in social groups and found that "talking is a tool for socially constructed thought, not just evidence of it.... What groups talk about in engaged ways and think about, they remember." Multimodal opportunities in exhibitions have also been linked to visitors' learning-styles and the likelihood for learning (Gardner 1983; Feher 1985; Hirschi and Screven 1988; Hilke, Hennings and Springuel 1988; Landay and Bridge 1982; Bitgood 1990b; Ogden et al. 1993). Both Davidson (1991) and Harvey et al. (1995) found that interactive and multisensory exhibits elicited more focused concentration and engagement by visitors, although Alt and Shaw (1984) advise that interactivity alone is not a guarantee of success. To avoid "five common pitfalls" of science center interactives, Allen and Gutwill (2004) offer design solutions based on their experiences at the Exploratorium. Finally, researchers suggested that visitors with differing prior knowledge and experience can all be reached to enhance learning (Koran, Koran and Foster 1988; Ogbu 1995; Gardner 1983.).

Research Relevant to Reinforcing Experiences

The works of Csikszentmihalyi (1990) and Csikszent-mihalyi and Hermanson (1995a,b) define intrinsic motivations for learning, demonstrating that such factors as clear goals, appropriate rules, immediate and unambiguous feedback, and tasks that are doable yet provide stimulation increase the likelihood of learning–and these are many of the aspects of a reinforcing experience. Other resources support those features and their relationships to positive learning environments (Hermann and Plude 1995; Evans 1995; Chambers 1990). Hedge (1995) says, "Redundancy refers to the fact that only about 20 percent of written language is actually required for us to extract meaning...but the rest...provides additional contextual cues that help to shape and reinforce correct interpretation."

Information overload, whether because of too many artifacts or verbose labels, has long been known to inhibit time spent and amount of material focused on (Melton 1935; Evans 1995; Hedge 1995; Falk and Dierking 1992; Derryberry 1941; Borun 1980; Crane, Nicholson, Chen, and Bitgood 1994.)

Exhibits that are "easy to understand" have been linked to the potential for learning (Griggs 1993; Jarrett 1986; Feher and Rice 1985, Serrell 1981). Griggs (1983) addressed the importance of a coherent environment in which ideas are both reinforced and complementary, as does Hedge (1995). Psychologists have shown that memory can be improved by "chunking the bits into pieces meaningful to the learner," and that it is strongly dependent on the nature and organization of the information (Branstord et al. 1986). Hilke demonstrated (1988) that content is best learned when it is integrated into exhibition themes.

References on Meaningfulness

Csikszentmihalyi's work on flow and intrinsic motivation indicates that natural motivation to learn can be kindled by meaningful activities and the ability to "discover aspects of oneself that were previously unknown" (Csikszentmihalyi 1990a,b; Csikszentmihalyi and Hermanson 1995a,b). Resources presented in Herrmann and Plude (1995) support these premises–and their own prescription for invoking "museum memory"–that is, to tell visitors why what they are seeing is important; to use music and language to elicit reverence in keeping with the topic; and telling visitors that having seen and learned about certain objects imparts status. Kintsch (1994) shows that to maximize learning, texts must overlap somewhat but not completely with what people know, thus leaving room for individual problem solving.

The relevance of the content, whether it be perceived personally or through effective communication, is linked by several researchers with the desire and ability to learn (Grunig 1980; Hirschi and Screven 1988; Jarret 1986; Kintsch 1994; Bransford et al. 1986), as is the ability of the material to reach people at any individual skill level or experience (Koran, Koran, and Foster 1988; Silverman 1995). One of the few studies of long-term satisfaction (Brown 1999) indicated that people had a greater inclination to support the institution after they had visited than they had beforehand.

Counter to the often-used marketing claim made by science museums that visitors will learn without even realizing that they are learning, the best learners are cognizant of their own learning strategies and experiences (Bransford 1979), suggesting that learners are acting consciously as they make meaning.

In *Listening in on Museum Conversations*, data gathered on visitors' discussions during and after exhibit visits suggested that visitors would be willing to engage with information that revealed the museum's meanings. "Visitors seem prepared to move to an understanding of the purpose of an object, the very act of deciding to show this object rather than another, and to emphasize one idea over another" (Leinhardt and Knutson 2004).

Studies done at Chicago's Brookfield Zoo on conservation behavior have concluded that specified factors in exhibitions can change people's behaviors in positive ways for a certain amount of time (Dotzour et al. 2002; Saunders et al. 1999). These include: incorporating familiar and unfamiliar behaviors; providing immediate and long-term opportunities for action; positively framing messages; providing opportunities for visitors to interact with each other; and providing repeated exposure to environmental messages.

I have encountered fierce resistance to valuing notions such as comfort and engagement. People who are not familiar with the visitor studies literature tend to think that these principles are merely a matter of taste or personal preference, at worst empty efforts to pander or entertain, and hence not seen as fundamental to museum learning.

Dan Spock

Resources across All Four EJ Criteria

The sources below relate to more than one of the Excellent Judges Criteria, and many contain helpful bibliographies.

Falk and Dierking (1995) edited an important post-conference source book called *Public Institutions for Personal Learning*. All of the articles reframe factors that enhance or increase the opportunity for learning and come with extensive bibliographies.

In particular, Alan Hedge (1995) presents issues on comfort and reinforcement from his field of human factors and ergonomics. Gary Evans (1995) does the

same for environmental psychology and the impacts on cognitive fatigue, including references to issues of comfort, engagement, and reinforcement. Herrmann & Plude (1995) present a fascinating approach to "museum memory," including material from the psychological literature on engagement and comfort. A survey of intrinsic motivation by Csikszentmihalyi and Hermanson (1995b) discusses the theoretical underpinnings for the importance of issues of comfort, reinforcement, and meaningfulness for human learning to take place, with an excellent bibliography.

Informal Science Learning: What the Research Says about Television, Science Museums, and Community-Based Projects, an edited volume by Crane, Nicholson, Chen, and Bitgood (1994), contains a discussion with bibliography of specific exhibition issues and their impact on learning, such as orientation, length of text, interactive devices, immersion, and time spent (Bitgood, Serrell, and Thompson 1994). The book contains an 80-page annotated bibliography of articles related to learning in museums.

Chandler Screven's valuable *Visitor Studies Bibliography and Abstracts* (1999) provides sources for impacts of orientation; interactivity; information overload; and personal relevance, from visitor studies in museums and from the behavioral and cognitive psychology literature.

Several articles by Bitgood (Bitgood 1990a; Patterson and Bitgood 1988) provide surveys of literature on effective label design and the relationship between visitor behavior and exhibit design, establishing the importance of factors that encourage visitors to become engaged and spend more time, two of the fundamentals for learning to take place. Alt and Shaw (1984) did a interesting study in the Hall of Human Biology at the British Museum of Natural History in London to discover the "characteristics of ideal museum exhibits" according to visitors. After interviewing nearly 2,000 people, their data revealed, among other things, the importance to visitors that exhibitions "make the subject come to life," "get the messages across quickly," and "have something in it for all ages."

In a fairly short, easy-to-read volume, *Learning in the Museum*, George Hein reviews what is known about learning in museum exhibitions. Jay Rounds reviews citations of journal articles and books published over the last several years, gathering evidence that "shows clear evidence that a core literature is in fact evolving in the field"; almost 15% of the publications directly relate to visitor studies and another 14% deal with learning theory (Rounds 2002).

We urge you to explore these references and let them inspire your own research or your exhibition development.

Meeting John R. Frederiksen

*Barbara Becker
contributed to this
chapter.*

To improve the effectiveness of science teaching, educational researcher John R. Frederiksen developed tests and assessments for teachers that "directly reflect and support the development of the aptitudes and traits they are supposed to measure" (Frederiksen et al. 1998) In Frederiksen's terminology, such tests and assessments are "systemically valid," because they demonstrate an improvement in those skills after the test or assessment has been in place for a period of time. Frederiksen has applied his systems-based theory to varied purposes such as creating standardized student tests, building "scientific inquiry projects" for teaching science skills, and assessing the performance of teachers in the classroom.

In the 1990s, Frederiksen was principal scientist for the Educational Testing Service (ETS) in Oakland, Calif., and also taught in the Education Department at the University of California at Berkeley. The techniques he developed, especially for performance assessments of mathematics teachers, provided good models for the Excellent Judges project. His assessment techniques

- incorporated direct and positive ways in which assessment could be used to improve teaching

- are based on "observable qualities," i.e., they were empirically generated and based upon actual observations of classroom teaching

- were practitioner-developed and independent of content and intent

120

- involved teachers in actively evaluating their own teaching
- were aimed to directly aid teachers in developing a classroom climate that fosters learning and understanding

Overall, the Excellent Judges objectives parallel those Frederiksen developed for his assessment of teachers.

Although we had been aware of Frederiksen's work from the beginning of the second EJ process in 2002, we didn't want to ask for his help until we had developed a framework of our own to show him. We didn't want to go to him and say, "What should we do?" Rather, we wanted to develop our tool first, working out a process that reflected our professional needs as we saw them, then go to him and ask, "What do you think?" In addition, in the earlier phases of the Framework development, we had less clarity about questions we needed to ask.

By the end of 2002, with the first version of the tool published, the grant awarded, and a second team of judges at work, we were ready. Beverly Serrell, Barbara Becker, Sue Allen, and John R. Frederiksen sat down together for a very productive four-hour conversation in Berkeley. He gave us valuable advice, much of which we followed.

John R. Frederiksen's ideas were very helpful and influenced our thinking.

No "Truth"

Frederiksen encouraged us to think of the Framework as a shared way to *talk about* excellence in exhibits, not to *define* it. He urged us to emphasize that the Framework is not a *truth*–that there is more than one way to construct such a tool.

Excellence itself is not a single "truth" that can be described. It changes and can be improved upon, the same as any teachers' curriculum and practice. There is no one right way to create excellence, nor to define the Framework; it is a concept built to be used. Instead, Frederiksen stressed the value of the Framework as a process for creating a shared vocabulary to reflect and improve upon our practice. In the spirit of true research, "It's whatever works and is interesting."

No One Likes to Be Judged

"Framework fears" are common to groups of professionals. The fears expressed by Frederiksen's teachers (and our fellow exhibition professionals) are that (1) a framework will force everyone to do things the same way; and (2) that they will be judged by those not sympathetic with their way of doing things, that is, (3) scorers might come in with different "theories" (or pedagogies) about their practice and judge everything from that one point of view.

People frequently confuse being judged personally with being assessed on their work or efforts. And work and efforts can always be improved upon. While it is difficult for human beings to overcome defensiveness, judging can lead to better practices, if all parties approach it with open minds.

To help work around these natural fear factors, Frederiksen stressed that the Excellent Judges Framework needs to focus on functions, not prescriptions. Our goal for assessments is to look for affordances, and this helps put the emphasis on judging the thing, not the person who made it.

Some people actually get to the point where they invite and actively solicit critical feedback from their peers. It's good to be able to take it as well as dish it out.

Hannah Jennings

Overcoming Fears and Resistance

The key to overcoming resistance to using the Framework and reducing the fear of being judged is having a good understanding of how the process works–through training and practice with peers. Peer training (as opposed to "expert" training) means that groups are encouraged to learn about and use the tool on their own, and to practice both assessing and being assessed. Peer training focuses interest on the professional development function of the Framework. It makes everyone an Excellent Judge.

Training and practice assure that the meanings and definitions of the Criteria are apparent to all practitioners: both assessors and those whose projects are being assessed. It assures that every player is aware of the things that their project can do to reach the next higher rating level. The Framework's inner workings become transparent.

Talking as a group about ratings and Rationales during the assessment process (social mediation of the ratings) is of critical importance. It reduces theoretical bias, or pedagogy, and maximizes fairness in the process of assessment.

What Should We Call It?

At the time we met with Frederiksen in 2002, we were calling our Framework a "tool," or "a tool for judging excellence." Frederiksen said that a tool implies something with which to "repair" a project, and suggested we call it a "framework." Also, instead of "judging," he suggested we use the word "assessment." Assessment is merely making observations, not passing down judgments. In addition, he encouraged us to eliminate the practice of "scoring." Instead, he suggested we use a rubric (a set of classes or categories), and let "excellence" be part of that rubric.

How We Applied Frederiksen's Ideas

We came back from our meeting in Berkeley with renewed vigor. Frederiksen's feedback helped us clarify our process and redefine some of our vocabulary, and it both reinforced and redirected our intentions. Having used his work as a model for ours, we'd shown it to him and listened to his reactions. Now we were ready to incorporate his ideas and suggestions and move forward.

We adopted his use of the term "systemic validity" and stopped searching for statistical validity. We relaxed our expectations for reliability. We started

I suspect we will never be able to account for all personality differences. Some people are open to critique; others are not; and many of us will be more or less open depending on the circumstances.

Eugene Dillenburg

calling it a framework instead of a tool. We dropped the notion of scoring, and began developing a rubric–words instead of numbers. We completely abandoned the use of total scores. But we kept separate ratings for each of the Criteria to reveal and emphasize differences where they existed instead of averaging scores, which tended to obscure disagreements. We gave up the intention of using the EJ Framework to compare exhibitions and focused on discussing them one at a time, as individual case studies.

We took a lot of his advice, but not all of it. We continued to use the words "judge," "excellent," "rating," "tool," and the double-whammy "excellent judges." Why? Our profession tends to be characterized mostly by polite reviews, criticism given behind backs, and few shared guidelines. We wanted to use language that was stronger and clearer. Judging implies standards against which something is being judged, and the Framework's Criteria and Aspects provided the necessary structure for making such judgments.

Issues with Validity and Reliability

When we first started the Framework project, we were interested in creating a statistically reliable and valid tool for judging excellence in exhibitions. As we evolved our categories and tried out various versions of the Framework, we discovered there were different definitions of "validity" and different interpretations of "reliability." In the end, we decided that, by the strictest academic research standards, those qualities were neither achievable nor desirable, and we would certainly benefit from more contextual definitions for our particular situation. So the question changed from "Is the Framework valid and reliable?" to "What kinds of validity and what amount of reliability is important to us?"

Sue Allen contributed to this chapter.

Systemic Validity, Construct Validity, and Predictive Validity

The most basic definition of validity is the degree to which a particular test or measurement tool assesses what you intend it to. Systemic validity, construct validity, and predictive validity are three different kinds of validity that are relevant and authentic for the Framework's use.

First, let's consider systemic validity. In the current school system, there are contentious issues about the validity of standardized multiple-choice tests. People see them as not being valid because they often do not measure the skills that the curriculum or teacher was supposed to teach, but instead measure students' ability to take the test. In high-stakes situations for students and teachers (e.g., advancing a grade level, getting into college, earning merit pay), entire subcultures may emerge to teach students skills for succeeding on those particular tests.

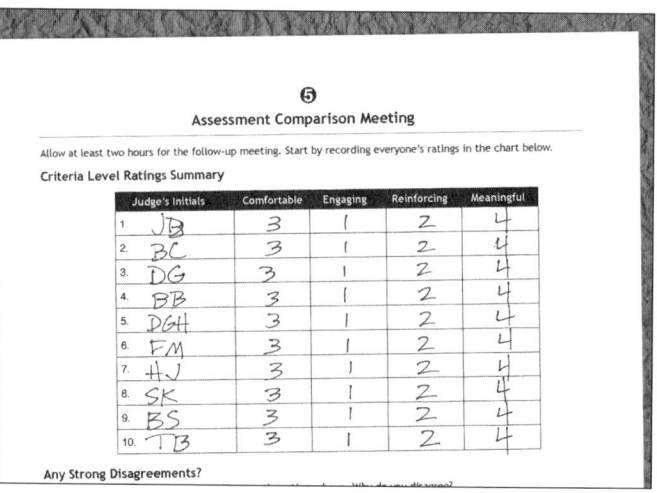

⑤

Assessment Comparison Meeting

Allow at least two hours for the follow-up meeting. Start by recording everyone's ratings in the chart below.

Criteria Level Ratings Summary

Judge's Initials	Comfortable	Engaging	Reinforcing	Meaningful
1. JB	3	1	2	4
2. BC	3	1	2	4
3. DG	3	1	2	4
4. BB	3	1	2	4
5. DGH	3	1	2	4
6. FM	3	1	2	4
7. HJ	3	1	2	4
8. SK	3	1	2	4
9. BS	3	1	2	4
10. TB	3	1	2	4

Any Strong Disagreements?

Perfect agreement among judges on their ratings for all four Criteria was never achieved or, as we found out, expected.

However, instead of dismissing this behavior as undesirable or cheating, there's another way to look at it. What if the criteria of the test were actually recognized as important and valuable? Then "teaching to the test" could be seen as a positive, dynamic system in which the assessment techniques cause feedback to the teaching procedures, which in turn cause a change in the methods that results in higher scores for the learners. The assessment drives the entire system in increasingly productive directions. This is defined as systemic validity, according to educational researchers John Frederiksen and Alan Collins (1989). They say a systemically valid test is "one that induces in the education system curricular and instructional changes that foster the development of the cognitive skills that the test is designed to measure." They further explain, "Evidence for systemic validity would be an improvement in those skills after the test has been in place within the educational system for a period of time." Well, what if there were an assessment technique for museum exhibitions that caused feedback to make more excellent exhibitions and more engaged visitors? That would be the essence of systemic validity.

126

Systemic validity applies perfectly to the kind of assessment system of the Framework, because its goals are at the systemic level. "The long-term goal of this research was to improve the quality of visitors' experiences in science museum exhibitions," was our statement on the EJ Web site from Day 1. This is a clear statement that the project sees exhibition assessment as part of a larger dynamic system of exhibition development and use, and that the EJ developers intended the final ratings of exhibitions to serve as feedback to future design. As a tool for professional development, the validity of the Framework should be measured not just in isolation (Did these judges really measure the comfort level of this exhibition?) but in a larger systemic context: If we adopt these Criteria within the field, and assess for them, and then use the feedback to change what we do, will we end up building exhibitions that actually afford better learning opportunities for visitors? To actually test the systemic validity of the EJ Framework in this way would be a huge endeavor, requiring longitudinal study of the changes in exhibit development over a period of years. This would be a worthwhile project.

Frederiksen and Collins provided a list of the general characteristics that contribute to the systemic validity of a testing system, and many of the same characteristics appear in the Excellent Judges project. Specifically, the system has

- a representative set of tasks (in this case, various existing educational exhibitions)
- a small number of primary criteria (the Framework has four)
- a training system for learning to score exhibitions (Step 1 of the Framework process)
- opportunities for repeated scoring and practice in self-assessment by practitioners as well as judges (repeated use of the Framework by a group of judges, e.g., peers, in-house staff, or museum studies students)
- a library of exemplars

The main component in Frederiksen and Collins' list that has not yet been incorporated by the EJ project to support its systemic validity is the creation of a library of exemplars. In schools, Frederiksen was able to do this because it was not a problem to videotape a teacher in a classroom as he or she presented a concept or an activity. Viewing the tape at a later date to see what happened was still a relatively authentic experience. Not so with self-guided exhibitions. Creating exemplars has been a challenge for the EJ project because of the holistic and experiential nature of being a visitor in an exhibition. There is no way to re-create an exhibition in a video or a series of photographs. Exhibitions are meant to be visited in three dimensions and real time. The closest we've come is to show individual exhibit elements in photographs, relate them to judges' Call-outs, and link the Call-outs to the related Aspects of the Criteria. We can show examples of those bottom-up building blocks, but the Framework ultimately judges the entire exhibition and rates the Criteria for the experience as a whole.

Construct validity, another form of validity, is the agreement on which important characteristics or Criteria of the Framework are to be measured and how they are defined. The EJ team worked long and hard at coming up with the Criteria and Aspects now seen in the Framework. It was a milestone to agree on what the Criteria were and subsequently apply them to many exhibitions. Construct validity of the Criteria was improved through many discussions of different examples. This is not to say that the Framework's Criteria were the only ones possible, but there was consensus that, for this group's purposes, they were comprehensive and important. In the context of a direct, holistic performance assessment system such as the EJ Framework, Frederiksen defines validity as the degree to which there is "a clear, socially shared meaning for each of the scoring criteria used by the judges" (Frederiksen et al. 1998). This we have.

Yet another form of validity that is appropriate here is the extent to which the ratings of judges using the EJ tool correlate with evaluation studies of the same exhibition. This is called predictive validity–discovering the extent to which the EJ ratings predict the results of related measures of the visitor experience. We have seen, in fact, that Framework judgments are similar to findings from summative visitor studies. But there are few one-to-one comparisons since summative studies often look for very different forms of evidence for success–often related to specific, unique communication goals, and dealing with content, not widely applicable affordances. For example, these were some evaluation study purposes:

- For *Milky Way*: to assess visitors' use of and experience with the Milky Way Galaxy; to document the scope of the gallery's impact and effectiveness (Randi Korn & Associates 1999).

- For *Genetics*: to learn about the ways in which and extent to which the exhibit meets its goals (Selinda Research Associates 2003) and to measure visitors' attention to the main messages of the exhibition (Institute for Learning Innovation 2003)

- For *Play It Safe*: to present evidence for the ways in which the exhibition's objectives were met (Serrell & Associates 2003).

If the criteria of the summative evaluation were structured to include more of the Aspects of the Framework, we expect there would be a high correlation between the issues raised by the judges and the responses seen by visitors and reported in evaluation reports, because the Framework is grounded in trends from 50 years of visitor studies.

Consistency of Ratings

Reliability is the degree to which ratings are consistent across time and among different judges, and it is a desirable trait for any form of assessment. The usual way to test for reliability in subjective assessments is

> *To the extent that judges do come to a shared understanding of the Criteria through discussion of multiple examples, they have moved the field forward, giving us a common language to talk about our craft.*
>
> Sue Allen

to have multiple coders compare their scores and then measure the degree of disparity among them. A reliable assessment is one with a high degree of agreement among judges looking at the same performance (in this case, an exhibition). With direct, holistic performance assessment, reliability is usually the greatest challenge because there is so much subjectivity involved in rating a specific example according to a set of broad criteria.

During this project, the EJ team's reliability never achieved the 90% level that would be required to consider the Criteria as reliable constructs from an *academic* perspective, but we decided that this level of agreement was not of critical importance for several reasons. First, the idea of measuring excellence turned out to be even more of an elusive goal than we'd originally suspected. Second, we subsequently shifted our emphasis from achieving reliability of a measurement instrument to creating a useful professional development tool, wherein disagreements were seen as useful components of a discussion, not a drawback. Finally, extensive training and further refinements of the Framework to try to achieve higher reliability were not feasible logistically within the scope of the project. Although we had the same group of judges visiting multiple exhibitions, we kept modifying the Framework as we tested it. We suspect that continued training with a group of assessors working with a uniform version of the Framework might lead to more similar scores, as it did with Dillenburg's museum studies students (see page 81). If the tool were to be used in the future for a high-stakes purpose such as rating competing exhibitions for awards, high reliability would be more important to ensure that the ratings were meaningful and not arbitrary.

High reliability has been achieved in judging complex performances on a variety of topics. For example, the National Assessment of Educational Progress (NAEP) has developed a system for holistic assessment of essay writing, where agreement among judges ran between 91% and 95%. In a meeting of well-trained, experienced essay judges at the Educational Testing Service, the ratings of essays by a room full of people showed almost no disagreements at all. Sue Allen, who observed this, said one the judges commented, "Once you get used to scoring the essays, telling the different grades apart is like telling a nickel from a dime from a quarter—you just look at them and it's obvious."

Frederiksen's study of math teachers (1998) showed that reliability was significantly improved by practice, as well as by "social moderation," in which the judges shared their initial ratings and rationales, and attempted to reach agreement. This improvement in reliability isn't surprising: With consensus as the goal, the judges' meanings of the terms gradually aligned with each other. This might seem like some form of cheating or weeding out of contrary opinions, but in fact it can move the field forward. The alignment signifies a group of people coming to a shared understanding of what we mean in practice by important terms like "meaningfulness," which are often used but seldom defined. The EJs also engaged in this kind of social moderation, and it is a recommended part of the process.

Perhaps a more extended project with more time for training would have put high reliability within the EJ's grasp. On the other hand, achieving high reliability may simply be unfeasible. Even Frederiksen's math team at Educational Testing Service achieved a maximum of only 71% agreement on its criteria, and that was following social moderation. Frederiksen interpreted this as implying that the judges were still on a learning curve at the end of their teacher assessment project. There are several features that might make inter-judge agreement even more difficult for the EJs.

- There is much greater diversity of audience in an exhibition than in a mathematics classroom, making it more difficult to agree on the "visitor perspective."

- In a classroom, it is possible to witness directly the immediate impact of instructional techniques and

131

interventions on the entire intended audience. This helps one to judge the effectiveness of an educational strategy because of evidence from the learner side as well as the teacher side. But in exhibitions, the intended audience is temporally spread out, so judging the effectiveness of a certain strategy to an equivalent degree would require watching many diverse groups of visitors use each part of the exhibition–a lengthy, even unfeasible task.

- The field of exhibition design does not have a group of universally acknowledged "masterful builders" in the same way as "masterful teachers" are recognized in the teaching community. This makes disagreements more likely because all judges' perspectives are seen as equally valid.

Some of our best research at the Exploratorium has been motivated by staff disagreements about whether certain techniques are effective with visitors or not.

Sue Allen

Another argument against the need for high reliability with the Framework is in the way the results of the judging are used. There is no grade or report. No one loses his job or gets a promotion on the basis of the judges' assessment. *The value lies in being a judge and participating in the process.* If the exhibition being assessed by a group of EJs is one that you helped develop, then there is added value in having very concrete, thoughtful comments from peers about your work. You can see and hear the ratings and Rationales given by each judge. You get your own opinions reinforced, challenged, or maybe even changed.

Given the numerous challenges of achieving high reliability, the EJs chose to refocus the project goals on creating a tool for professional development. Even if the judges disagree in their ratings of an exhibition, there is value in hearing each other's interpretations and recognizing that different points of view are possible. Such disagreements may also identify hot areas for future evaluation and visitor research.

Wild Reef:
A Points-of-View Case Study

In the course of developing the Framework, the Chicago team visited 16 exhibitions. In six cases, we had access to the museums' summative evaluation reports for the exhibitions, so there was an opportunity after the EJ process to make direct comparisons between the findings of the evaluation studies and our discussions.

Eugene Dillenburg contributed to this chapter.

The contents of the reports were not easily aligned with the judges' discussions, however, because the evaluation reports focused mainly on visitors' understanding of the exhibit communication goals and did not attempt to assess the same Criteria as the Framework. The report for Shedd Aquarium's *Wild Reef* (Beaumont 2005) was unusual in that it contained more visitor-centered aspects as opposed to concentrating on message outcomes. Thus, it lent itself to comparison with the Excellent Judges findings.

Wild Reef is an immersion habitat exhibition of a Philippines coral reef with fishes, including sharks. It makes an interesting case study because one of the original EJs, Eugene Dillenburg, was lead developer for the exhibition. When the EJs tried out the September 30, 2003 version of the Framework to judge *Wild Reef,* he saw it as a chance to see the exhibition through fresh, unbiased eyes. Dillenburg sat in on the

133

EJ discussion as "a fly on the wall"—not participating, just listening. None of the judges knew of his involvement in the exhibit.

One of the developers of *Wild Reef* got to listen in as a group of Excellent Judges discussed their experiences there. In about half of the exhibitions the EJs visited, a "stakeholder" was involved in the process.

What follows is a very brief summary of (1) the judges' findings for each Criterion, along with (2) some of the findings from the summative evaluation conducted for Shedd; (3) Dillenburg's candid comments about the exhibition's interpersonal dynamics, institutional politics, and the oftentimes-contentious effort that produced it—issues not unfamiliar to many experienced exhibit developers; as well as (4) some more-generalized notions and observations on the field by Beverly Serrell and her attempts to turn them into lessons learned. These comments are grouped by the Framework's four Criteria of Comfortable, Engaging, Reinforcing, and Meaningful.

Comfort in *Wild Reef*

THE JUDGES: The judges found the exhibit less than comfortable: a single entrance (down an elevator), poor orientation to the space, narrow pathways, and lack of adequate seating.

Summative Evaluation: The summative study revealed problems with orientation, crowding, and a lack of adequate seating.

Dillenburg: *Most of these issues had come up during planning, but no one took "ownership" of them. We were all intent on our design and development plans, and we jettisoned comfort when it got in our way. Visitor comfort is everyone's responsibility; we should have worked harder to achieve it.*

Serrell: We have noticed that one bad experience in an exhibition can cast a negative pall over the whole show. It makes you think about all the little things that are wrong (broken interactives, elements not put in yet, a missing label) that you haven't taken care of, and there are hundreds of visitors putting up with them— or maybe not.

Engagement in *Wild Reef*

The Judges: The judges found the faux reef wonderfully engaging in a physical/visual sense, calling it "astounding" and "mind-blowing." They also noted, however, that intellectual engagement was lacking. Labels were sometimes blocked by surface treatments, other times out of eyesight overhead. Interpretive elements were often "overwhelmed" by the design. They "could not compete." Design served design, but not so much the messages.

Summative Evaluation: The evaluator reported that visitors were very impressed with the exhibition's immersive design, overwhelmingly so. A surprising number of people commented directly on aspects of lighting, acoustics, size, Plexiglas. They also liked the sharks, the big tanks, the diversity of life on the reef.

Dillenburg: *As a developer, I gained a new respect for the power of design. But I also learned the importance of making design and content work together. An exhibit cannot promote one to the detriment of the other.*

SERRELL: Engagement was often the Criterion that got the most favorable ratings from judges for other exhibitions as well. Our profession has learned lots of ways to engage visitors–from colorful computer-generated graphics, to computer-based interactives, to large-screen high-quality video productions, to simple-but-effective mechanical, low-tech interactive devices. What we have not learned so well is how to provide more comfortable, reinforcing and meaningful experiences.

Reinforcement in *Wild Reef*

THE JUDGES: In addition to the physical problems with the interpretation noted above, the judges found the gallery conceptually "disjointed" and "confusing." For example, the exhibit is about coral, yet it begins on a beach where no coral lives. Most seriously, the story of people's relationship with the reef seemed to be relegated to the end rather than integrated throughout, and it seemed "tacked on."

SUMMATIVE EVALUATION: Most visitors, according to the report, did not get the intended "journey" or story line of the interpretation. The last area with the human connections was the least popular and less memorable than the sharks and the exhibit environment.

DILLENBURG: *I feel primarily vindicated. Some of us on the team had fought against these approaches very strongly, only to be overruled.*

SERRELL: Sounds like a contentious process based on a weak Big Idea to me, resulting in an uncohesive presentation. It's a common situation.

136

Meaningfulness in *Wild Reef*

THE JUDGES: Given these problems with the interpretation, the judges did not rate the exhibition high on meaningfulness. Some did mention messages they had stumbled across, stating, "This was an important point that should have received more play."

SUMMATIVE EVALUATION: Evaluation showed that visitors picked up on messages about conservation, diversity, and interconnectedness, but they were most impressed with the design.

DILLENBURG: *Again, many on the team had worried that the richly designed environment would overwhelm the meaning, and according to the judges, that's exactly what happened.*

SERRELL: It is interesting to see how the visitors and the judges had similar reactions to the immersive design: It was the most impressive and memorable part of the exhibition. Visitors were largely satisfied with that experience and did not look for a deeper meaning or feel that the exhibition was lacking something. The EJs, on the other hand, were sharply critical of the exhibition's missed opportunities to afford more meaningful experiences beyond the immediate and superficial "wow" of the theatrical environment.

We also note that conservation, diversity, and interconnectedness are the main themes of many other zoo and aquarium exhibitions and are the topics often covered in other media featuring interesting wildlife. It is not surprising, therefore, that visitors to *Wild Reef* "learned it."

Keeping your mouth shut about the intent and constraints you worked under is a challenge, but it leads to open discussion of the sort you never hear about your own exhibit work. You can always tell the group why you made the design decisions you made after the discussion is over.

Hannah Jennings

Comparing the Framework to Evaluation Findings

Judges, like other visitors, were attracted to large interactive exhibit elements. Judges, unlike visitors, looked deeper into what the interactivity afforded overall.

The case study above is tantalizing because of parallels with what judges and other visitors react to, and we noticed other cases where the judges agreed with visitor feedback. This is hardly surprising since the judges are visitors and are actively looking for evidence of engaging, reinforcing, meaningful experiences. Commonalities often occurred between judges and other visitors as to the most popular elements in the exhibition (live animals, engaging interactive components, large elements) and the most problematic areas (sound bleed, broken exhibits, confusing elements).

Differences between what the judges discussed and what visitor feedback said came in the depth of the analysis. The judges went beyond the surface of the experience (things to look at, do and learn, "it was cool") to what the underlying meaning of the experiences were or could be. For example:

- In *Play It Safe* at the Chicago Children's Museum, visitors understood that the exhibits were about safety in the home, preventing dangerous situations, and what to do in emergencies. Judges articulated the same things, and added that it could have been more about safety as a way of thinking. They were also concerned that the exhibits did not adequately address affect: that is, visitors' anxieties or fears about dangers (e.g., fire, poison, pornography).

- In *Underground Adventure* (a 15,000-square-foot exhibition about soil biology) at the Field Museum, judges and visitors enjoyed the mega-sized animatronics but missed having experiences with real dirt. The judges went on to say that the "underground" portion and the Soil Lab were two unrelated experiences, that it felt way too clean, and perhaps the subject did not warrant such a large amount of real estate.

- In *Genetics: Decoding Life*, a new exhibition at the Museum of Science and Industry in Chicago that includes the iconic hatching-chicks display, summative evaluation reported that visitors overall were very positive about their experiences during post-visit interviews. They found it "interesting," "informative," and "educational." Both visitors and judges were put off by issues of high noise levels and a few nonfunctioning exhibits. Judges' Call-outs, on the other hand, were largely critical and negative, e.g., "frustrated," "confused," and "disappointed," with this admittedly difficult topic. Their negativity stemmed largely from many incidences in which an initially attracting exhibit did not prove to be a good experience. Judges went from feeling intrigued to feeling irritated. Perhaps visitors are less likely to report this level of disappointment.

Judges do tend to be more critical. Although the Framework's Criteria and Aspects are written in positive language, it is easy to notice confusing elements, annoying design features, or missed opportunities for a more engaging and meaningful experience.

The comparison question, on the surface, seems reasonable: If the Framework assesses exhibits for their positive learning affordances, and if summative evaluations measure visitors' actual positive learning experiences, wouldn't you expect to see lots of similarities in the findings from both methods of reviewing an exhibition? But the task of comparing evaluation reports with the judges' findings on a broader, more systematic scale was beyond the scope of the EJ project for several other reasons:

- First, the reports varied greatly in their methods, purposes, and authors. Most evaluation studies are primarily geared to answer the question, Did the exhibition meet its communication objectives? These objectives tend to be unique for each exhibition. Different evaluators favor different measures and forms of analysis, such as "knowledge hierarchies" (Selinda Research Associates 2002, 2003), pre- and post-interview comparisons (Saunders and Perry 1997), or quantified interview responses (Institute for Learning Innovation 2003).

- Second, the answers to the question above are not quantified in such a way as to allow comparisons between exhibitions at different museums.

- Third, the timing of our access to the reports varied. We did not have each one in hand when we were ready to visit or discuss them.

Thus, the task of comparing Excellent Judges findings with evaluation findings in a systematic way would require different museums to use the same evaluation methods and report their findings in similar ways. Even the widely shared methods of tracking and timing (unobtrusive observations of visitor behaviors) and the resultant comparable measures across exhibitions of "sweep rates" and the "percentage of diligent visitors" (Serrell 1998) have not been correlated with visitor-learning outcomes among different exhibitions, although there are strong correlations *within* an exhibition (i.e., longer times spent are indicative of greater learning outcomes). Shared-methods research is feasible and could be the subject of a future project.

Pivotal Moments in the History of Building the Framework

A number of pivotal moments defined the Excellent Judges project and process:

Being Positive

We realized almost at once that it was easier to note negative Call-outs in exhibitions than positive ones. We had to work hard at noticing and recording good Aspects as well as missed opportunities. We soon perceived that even though our discussions often focused on negative statements, we also could end up agreeing on many positive Aspects of an exhibition.

Bottom-up Approach

We had started working with an intellectual top-down approach, asking "What criteria are important?" Then we put the criteria aside and went into exhibitions asking the affective question, "How am I feeling and responding in here?" The protocol outlined in the Framework follows the bottom-up approach of thinking about how the exhibits affect you emotionally, which is authentically visitor-centered. The Call-outs are personal, while the Criteria are shared. We found that this process provided a balanced experience. Using the Framework helps people think beyond their superficial reactions in a structured way.

* state as affordances, not what you see
visitors doing

③ Exhibits are ~ing

c. Visitors seem to be engaged emotionally. — ing Leave in (Discuss)

as is

ⓔ d. Experiences come in a variety of formats and a variety of sensory modalities
- visual, auditory, textual, motion, touch, etc. — add Hannah's starting point

Ⓕ on Hannah's "g"

Exhibits provide opportunity to be successful

abundant for visitors with

3. Competence--In an excellent exhibition, visitors feel intellectually competent.
Competence is a cognitive comfort that goes beyond accessibility. The experiences
provide successful

easy

BB's

Ⓔ a. Visitors were not overwhelmed (although they may have been challenged).

— Insert BC's Ⓓ

a.

b. Visitors feel stimulated emotionally and intellectually, not numb, bored, or
anxious. There was "just enough" things to do.

move to Comfort

I can do this

as definition

c. The exhibit speaks to them.

arrange logically   is arranged   intellectually in a way that   Intellectual success

d. The presentation holds together and can be easily followed and understood.

It makes the subject come to life.   oh I get it the point

**4. Meaningfulness--An excellent exhibition is personally meaningful to visitors.
Beyond being engaged, visitors find themselves involved in immediate and long-
lasting ways.**

a. Ideas and objects of the exhibit (natural specimens, living collections, cultural
artifacts, demonstrations and activities) are relevant to the visitors. Visitors can
find personal connections.

relate with

are made relevant to

b. Visitors can learn something new, or make a new connection. They can say "I
never knew..., I didn't realize..., What if?..."

presented and
with appropriate

c. The information and ideas are reduntantly reinforced in a variety of different
formats.

d. It doesn't shy away from deep or controversial issues. The exhibit is more than
fun facts or boring, safe, or uncontroversial topics.

add Hannah's
Ⓕ includes
2

e. The exhibit experience changes them, moving them to new actions, beliefs.

The exhibit content builds on itself.

142

A Graphic Solution

We had what seemed like endless discussions about the Framework not being a checklist. On numerous occasions people tended to overlook the importance of thinking about exhibitions from a simple emotional point of view and responding to it with more words that express and analyze their feelings–the Call-outs. We finally arrived at a solution in the graphic layout of the Framework: Two blank, unlined pages, titled "Create Call-Outs," gave that step the prominence it deserved. As the EJs used the new format, they found it easy to follow the protocol, spending the experiential time to think probingly and write abundant notes on those two pages. Instructions that told you to do it were less effective than the graphic format that made it obvious. (This is also true for designing exhibits: We *should* know this.)

Editing, Editing, Editing

Through many revisions, edits, and discussions, we reduced the number of Criteria from five to four, changed the name and definition of one significantly, and rearranged the order. (The original five Criteria and sequence were: Comfort, Competence, Engagement, Meaningful, and Satisfaction; the final four are Comfortable, Engaging, Reinforcing, and Meaningful.)

Seemingly small semantic changes had thought-provoking results. The shift from Comfort (something that a visitor might feel) to Comfortable (an experience that can be afforded by the exhibition) helped us move away from evaluating visitors (which can't really be done right without talking to them) to assessing the exhibitions. This, in turn, allowed us to change "Competence" ("visitors felt competent") to Reinforcing (the exhibit afforded ways to reinforce a visitor's sense of competence).

We made the same shift away from using the word "visitor" in the Aspects to talking about the exhibit elements. Instead of saying, "Visitors feel stimulated emotionally and intellectually, not numb, bored or anxious," we say, "Exhibits were fun–pleasurable, challenging, amusing, intriguing, and intellectually or physically stimulating."

Another subtle but important edit: We eventually changed all Aspects to past tense rather than present tense, emphasizing the experience in the exhibition at the moment of the assessor's visit. This was how it was when the judge was on site. Things might get out of date, get fixed, or change in other ways when another judge was there.

The Answer to the Research Question

In review, the research question was: If different museum professionals used the same set of standards to review the same group of exhibitions, would their reviewers agree on the degree of excellence for each of the exhibitions? And if not, why not?

And the answer was: It took many iterations to come up with a set of standards that the group agreed on; we ended up scoring individual Criteria instead of the whole exhibition; and some judges did not agree on their ratings of a Criterion because they experienced the exhibition differently. Overall, we valued the discussions of our differences as well as our agreements, and the actual scores were of less importance.

The Criterion about reinforcement is the one that still generates the most discussion: Does it refer to the visitor or to the exhibition? Both. Should the portions of Reinforcing that are about the visitor be moved to the Meaningful Criterion? Maybe. We realize that this process could literally go on *ad infinitum*, but we have seen that the current Criteria are serving our purpose.

Valid But Not Reliable

Our discussions with educational researcher Dr. John R. Frederiksen and our testing of the Framework led us to conclude that the tool is valid but not reliable. And that is okay. As we experimented with different versions of the Framework, people agreed on the importance and relevance of the Criteria and what was being judged (high validity) but they were not always in agreement as to how those qualities were represented in an exhibition (low reliability). Since the tool is not being used to make any critical decisions (e.g., who gets hired or fired), this duality is not a hindrance to the tool's use. Consensus is not necessarily the goal of the discussion.

Paradigm Shift in Purpose

We had originally sought to develop a valid and reliable tool for judging excellence. As our talks progressed, the Framework evolved, and as we saw the benefits of disagreement, we realized the quest for a statistically reliable instrument was not within our grasp. However, we did have a powerful tool for professional development. We changed our focus from judgments that could help us compare exhibitions to assessments that could help us make better exhibitions.

Ratings

Related to our shift in purpose, scoring and rating approaches changed. We started with one score to summarize and compare whole exhibitions, then threw out that reductionist approach in favor of ratings and Rationales for each Criterion—as discussion starters, not final rulings. The rating rubric has six levels (1= Excellent). We chose to have the best score represented by the lowest number so that "1" would always mean "best" regardless of the number of levels being used. We defined "agreement" among judges to be a two-point spread.

Risk

We encountered risk-taking in our process. Judging is not looked on as a favorable activity by many museum professionals. The exhibit being judged is in a risky position (Faults revealed! Missed opportunities discussed openly!), and the judges take risks exposing themselves as people with opinions that might not be popular (You'll never work in this town again!). It is essential to emphasize that any risks associated with participating in the Framework were far outweighed by the benefits.

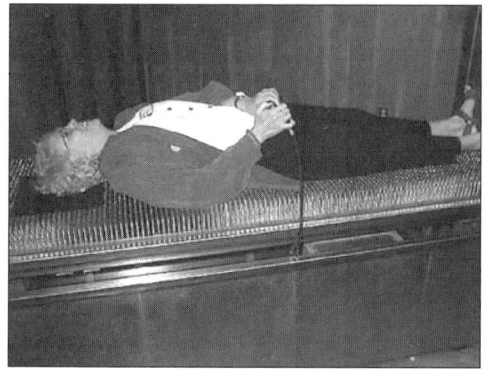

Just as a bed of nails looks more threatening than it turns out to be, so is judging exhibitions with the Framework.

PART V

THE FUTURE OF THE FRAMEWORK

The grant-funded portion of the EJ project has been over since 2003. The Excellent Judges Web site has continued to provide a reference for the history of the process and a downloadable copy of the Framework. We'd birthed it, and now it had a life of its own as people used it in many different ways. What factors might keep it alive? Below we will discuss why the Framework was so successful and how other forms of assessment can build on it; what a "library of exemplars" would consist of; and how the Framework can be used to improve communications within an institution.

Broader Use of Guidelines for Judging Excellence in Exhibitions

Seven advisors participated in the Excellent Judges project during the 18 months of the National Science Foundation funding. Each advisor was selected for different strengths–experience with exhibit development, science teaching in informal settings, visitor studies, and previous experience with working on NSF projects. Two advisors–Sue Allen and Joshua Gutwill–had several things in common: They both had been students at the University of California at Berkeley and had experience with educational researcher John R. Frederiksen, and they both had worked in the department of visitor research and evaluation at the Exploratorium in San Francisco, a hotbed of visitor studies for the past 10 years.

Sue Allen had an unusual perspective on the Excellent Judges project because she had participated in something similar before. While a graduate student at Berkeley, she worked with Frederiksen on a research project to identify excellence in mathematics teaching in public schools. Sue says, "At first it seemed like an impossible goal. Teaching is so personal, so dependent on the content being taught, the particular students, the style of the teacher, the goals of a particular lesson. How could we possibly create a general tool that could be used to assess mathematics teaching? It wasn't easy."

Sue Allen contributed to this chapter.

Many of the ideas from Frederikson's project informed the EJ's team, and, in turn, the characteristics of the Framework provide an excellent model for any other new assessment technique for looking critically at the quality of museum exhibitions. (See also the chapter Meeting John R. Frederiksen, pages 120 to 124.)

Key Characteristics Make the Excellent Judges Tool Valuable

Six main characteristics of the Framework establish its value: (1) it is holistic in nature; (2) its form of assessment is direct; (3) it represents key values for museum practitioners who (4) are interested in making visitor-centered educational experience in exhibitions; (5) it's a teaching tool; and (6) it's not exclusive—anyone can be a judge. Each of these characteristics, which have broad applicability to other tools, will be expanded on in the pages below.

It's a tool that has its own value system built in. You know the four categories—they're not my six or your three or something else. But all in all it's a pretty good set of values. It's a good way of creating the conversation. What came up today was a level of thinking about the exhibit that really pays off— something you can't just do on your own.

Robert Garfinkle

1. It's a form of holistic performance assessment.

Holistic performance assessment is a progressive form of assessment that judges the entire performance (in this case, the exhibition) as an integrated whole. This contrasts with more traditional reductionistic assessments that critique something by breaking it into smaller parts and running through a checklist of attributes that are relatively easy to measure.

For example, a reductionistic approach to assessing an exhibition might involve counting the number of elements that have fonts larger than 24 point (assuming this to be an indicator of accessibility), counting the number of references to community members (assuming this to be an indicator of community connection), or checking whether there is at least one map of the exhibition and a summary of its contents within 10 feet of the entry point (assuming this to be an indicator of successful orientation). Reductionistic assessment is relatively easy to conduct but tends to force everyone into a cookie-cutter approach, penalizing those who construct something novel and powerful that breaks many of the small, concrete rules.

By contrast, the EJ team used a holistic approach, putting their energies into defining broad Criteria (comfortable, meaningful, etc.) that can be applied to any exhibition. Because it doesn't specify any implementation details, the EJ system can handle much greater variations in exhibition design without becoming "unfair." The classic model of holistic performance assessment would be sports such as gymnastics or ice skating, where each performance is given a technical score and an artistic score. An important feature of this kind of assessment is that it does not require the competitors to perform identical tasks. In the case of ice skaters, different performers skate to different music and have unique choreography and costumes. In the case of the EJs, different exhibitions have different topics, sizes, layouts, emphases, audiences, and so on. Yet this Framework creates Criteria by which they can all be assessed.

2. The assessment is direct

A closely related issue to holistic performance assessment is the directness versus indirectness of an assessment. The Framework is a form of direct assessment, meaning that it directly measures what its designers regard as the "truly important" qualities of an exhibition (comfortable, meaningful, etc.). Most large-scale school assessments rely on indirect tests, consisting of long lists of simple items (such as multiple-choice tests) that are believed to correlate with what is "truly important" in the skills of the students. When deciding whether to use direct or indirect tests, many people immediately reject direct tests because of the subjectivity involved in rating a performance based on an abstract criterion such as comfort. Many progressive assessment experts have moved toward direct forms of measurement, especially in cases where a goal of the assessment is iterative learning by practitioners. The EJs directly assess the qualities of an exhibition that are considered desirable to the field, so there is no tricky correlational assumption between what is measured and what is concluded.

3. It articulates a set of key values for the field.

As practitioners, we devote our working lives to creating the best exhibitions we can, so "best" is at the heart of what drives us. But what *is* true excellence? This is not a theoretical question, but a question about actual physical exhibitions. How can we tell when we've created an excellent exhibition and when we haven't? Assessing excellence is at the intellectual heart of our field, but because is it so complicated and important, creating standards or criteria requires many voices and many iterations. The EJs have taken this on.

4. The Criteria are strong and visitor-centered.

After countless iterations and much deep discussion, the Criteria the EJs have created are understandable, comprehensive, of roughly equal scope, applicable to any educational exhibition, and important in the field. The four to eight Aspects that underlie each Criterion work well as links between the Criterion and observable qualities of an exhibition. By careful design, the framework focuses exclusively on the exhibition in

I see the main power of the Framework not in the ratings themselves, but in the collaborative process of constructing them. So I recommend withholding judgments about the usefulness of the tool until you've been in some of those discrepancy discussions with your colleagues and felt their energy.

Sue Allen

the final form seen by visitors, and the Criteria are grounded in decades of visitor studies research.

5. Learning comes from using the tool.

A wonderful side effect of holistic performance assessment such as the Framework is that genuine, powerful learning happens during the discussions of discrepancies among ratings. The beauty of this process is that, because the goal is a direct assessment based on Criteria that are seen as intrinsically important (such as Comfort or Meaningfulness), any arguments about how well a particular exhibition meets a Framework Criterion will be highly engaging and relevant to people's work. Far from being a waste of time, such arguments are the heart of a powerful professional development experience. Typically, the final ratings are less important than the process.

There is definitely a learning curve to using the Framework: Judges get better at it with experience, and the group dynamics become more complex among judges who have worked together.

6. Anyone can be an Excellent Judge.

The only requirement for being a judge is that one participate in the training. This means that the Framework is not about creating an elite group that presides over the rest of the field; rather, it is to empower all practitioners to think about their own and each other's work in a systematic way.

Many museum professionals have called for more criticism and thoughtful analysis of our exhibit products. As more people take on this challenge, they should incorporate the important and relevant qualities described here because they make criticism more productive.

Expanding the Functions of the Framework: Creating a Library of Exemplars

One of the questions or suggestions we heard from our peers during the development of the Framework was a request to see examples of excellence. People wanted to see specifics. We could certainly understand the desire for this, but for several reasons it was difficult to comply. The Framework is meant to be used *in situ*, as a full-body experience in a whole exhibition space. Considering an exhibition piecemeal would mean taking the parts out of context—yet context is so much the point of an exhibition experience. We were also reluctant to show examples because we feared that if we held up individual cases, people would see them as concrete prescriptions for what to do (or not do) rather than seeing the functions that they stood for.

A 2004 publication, *Are We There Yet? Conversations about Best Practices in Science Exhibition Development*, came about as a result of a conference held at the Exploratorium for museum professionals to discuss and share lessons learned in the field. In the book, "Twelve Noteworthy Science Exhibitions" are presented in pictures, narratives, and videos. These were not picked according to any set of criteria; they were deemed "exemplary" in a survey of exhibit practitioners for such characteristics as being innovative, having an unusual theme, or being interdisciplinary.

For example, the exhibition *Whodunit? The Science of Solving Crime* was cited for "its audience appeal, its immersive environment, and its marriage of market and mission" (McLean and McEver 2004). The term "exemplary" specifically avoided the issue of being "best" or "excellent" because the conference participants and authors of the book wanted to sidestep the problem of defining those terms. They said, "If we simply repeat what can be identified as 'best' today, we aren't reaching for the future. We ignore creativity and innovation. Should we not strive to do something *better* than we did before?"

The Framework does not present "Twelve Excellent Exhibitions" because the very nature of trying to define and identify excellence is a goal, not an end point. We strive for excellence; we have small successes in certain places; we have many missed opportunities, but we keep trying. And, by having a clear and valuable set of Criteria to use as a springboard for discussing that endeavor, we can constantly be creative and innovative with a shared understanding of where we are headed.

While we do not present a library of exemplars of excellence at the whole-exhibition level for each Criterion, and despite our reluctance to piecemeal, on the CD we do show a range of examples in photographs at the exhibit-element level. The photo captions on the CD are more extensive and interactive than in the book. They start with a bottom-up approach: first, there's a Call-out made by a judge as he or she visited the exhibition and wrote notes, reactions, and feelings. Next, on the CD, these Call-outs are linked to existing Aspects found in the Framework under each Criterion. A plus (+) for an Aspect means that the judge's Call-out represents the presence of the Aspect or evidence for the affordances. A minus (–) indicates evidence contrary to the desired Aspect, a missed opportunity. Note that these Call-outs are all written by individuals; it's not groupthink. In fact, one judge may have written a positive Call-out for the same exhibit element

for which another judge wrote a Call-out that cited a missed opportunity. The CD's photo captions include at least one example of every Aspect of each Criterion.

The CD is a far cry from creating a full library of exemplars–with multiple positive and negative examples of every Aspect of each Criterion. That would be a wonderful but difficult undertaking. Examples might take the form of still photos, video, or audio recordings–whatever most effectively shows the reader the element as the visitor would experience it. Such a collection of exemplars would ground the assessment in the real world, giving judges and practitioners (even casual ones visiting the project) a clearer idea of the range of performance possible on each Criterion, as well as some specific examples of excellence to bear in mind. The library would also provide a mechanism for increasing reliability across groups of judges.

Creating an appropriate library of exemplars would not be easy because of the logistical and representational difficulties of recording exhibitions that are diverse in sensory modalities, time scales, and spatial scales. How can you show an example that is primarily a kinesthetic experience? Is an exhibition that was excellent five years ago still excellent today, after five years of wear and tear?

Calibrating the Exemplars With Specific Evaluation Studies

If there were a library of exhibitions that became benchmarks for the field, then it might be helpful to do summative evaluation studies to calibrate the claims that these are examples of excellence (or lost opportunity), with respect to the Framework's Criteria. It would be worth investing the time to do this in order to choose benchmarks where evaluation studies support the ratings given by the EJs. As was mentioned early, this could be the topic of the next research project.

Furthermore, to strengthen the link between actual visitor responses and EJ ratings, it might be feasible to create and use evaluation instruments to gather visitor feedback that more closely matches the specific Criteria of the Framework. Although visitors may not be able to discuss the exhibition design features that led them to feel comfortable or stupid or deeply moved, they could probably tell you how they felt, especially at the whole-exhibition level. So another possible line of future development is the opportunity for visitors (cued, trained, and given substantial tokens of appreciation for their time) to rate their experiences on a quantitative scale similar to the Framework, as well as to comment on how they chose their ratings and which Aspects of the exhibition were most salient to them. This would be similar to the way judges write their Rationales.

Photographs on the CD are in color, and they are captioned with judges' Callouts, which are also linked with the related Aspects and Criteria of the Framework.

Bringing Staff Together for Better Communication, Efficiency and Outcomes

A museum director or director of public programs could use the Framework to generate shared values among as many museum staffers as possible. Curators, marketers, fund-raisers, educators, designers, production managers, and even engineers and architects could be encouraged to use the Framework to visit and assess exhibitions with the team. This would help to offset frustration levels that often increase as large-scale exhibition development projects drag on.

Clearly defining our terms will not end such debates, but it will force them out into the open, so that everyone understands what, exactly, is being debated.

When people from all departments have the experience of visiting and assessing exhibitions from a visitor-centered perspective, the sharing of vocabulary, ideals, and goals will be more likely. And it will then be *less* likely that needless sidetracking and revisions, caused by lack of understanding and agreement, will set back the process in either schedule or budget.

Professional training budgets are often strained or even nonexistent. The Framework can help here, too. Employers certainly cannot replace workshops, seminars, conferences, and other such training opportunities. But creating an EJ team and using the Framework regularly at work can broaden team members' awareness of exhibition issues without their leaving town. It can also deepen staff members' understanding of how they can contribute to creating innovative and successful exhibitions for visitors. By improving the individual employee's skill set, the institution as a whole benefits.

In the creative work of developing exhibitions, we need to embrace differences of opinions. Creative work considers differences and builds on them. In-house staff and consultants often gloss over disagreements or avoid conflict because they find it so uncomfortable. If people try to preserve relationships by not confronting differences, this "silencing conflict" can have negative results (Perlow 2003). The point is not about coming to agreement but about reaching new levels of mutual understanding. The Framework serves these goals.

After the ASTC Conference in Minnesota, at which we attended the Excellent Judges session, we came back to the office and told our colleagues about what we had seen and heard about the process. Our discussion raised subjects and issues we had never before articulated as a team—although we had been working together for more than a decade.

Margie Prager and Jeff Kennedy

Courage and Openness from the Field

There is no getting around the judgments involved in the Excellent Judges process, or any other holistic performance assessment. If every exhibition gets high ratings, the tool loses its effectiveness. It is precisely its ability to discriminate between excellence and lost opportunities that makes it useful and moves the field forward. Of course, this means that *someone's* exhibition has to be the exemplar of the lowest level of comfort or meaningfulness or engagement or anything else. This is especially difficult to ask of a field that is small and far from anonymous, where any exemplar could be traced easily to an institution or even a particular development team. But flawed examples of our work are often the most useful things we can share with our colleagues. How many of us would volunteer to post to a Web site our strongest and weakest examples based on the EJ Criteria so that others could benefit? How many of us are willing to listen when someone else critiques our work? It takes courage to share a judge's negative Call-outs or ratings, especially if you don't agree with them.

When the Excellent Judges look at an exhibition, they are looking for evidence of the Criteria and Aspects of the EJ Framework. They are not looking as individual critics with their own set of guidelines, or as consultants with a set of exhibition objectives to evaluate. The Framework provides a focus on affordances known to benefit visitor learning experiences.

What an investment more shared critiques would be in the learning of the field!

Sue Allen

Into the Future

Before ending, we need to stress that we are not by any means saying that those of us who have worked on exhibition teams were poorly intentioned or inattentive to the details that are called out in the Framework. We know from direct experience how intense and how complex the process of making an exhibition is and how easily things slip through the cracks.

Broad use of the Excellent Judges Framework inside institutions, and advocacy of its visitor-centered goals by exhibition professionals, just might make all of our jobs a bit easier–and the products of our efforts more effective–in the future.

Yes, exhibit development IS rocket science; it IS brain surgery.

Mike Spock

What If...?

Museums enjoy the public's trust, tax advantages as nonprofit institutions, and grants for developing, presenting, and traveling their exhibitions. Museums owe it to visitors, funders, and taxpayers to present the best practices in informal education through exhibitions. Consider this. What if all exhibit developers embraced the visitor-centered Framework and matched their intentions to it? What if exhibit developers shifted their attention from traditional communication goals to include content-free positive experiences that can be applied across a wide spectrum of exhibitions? Would that be so bad?

Glossary

Affordances are the opportunities that offer and enable excellent visitor learning experiences–experiences that should be available in an exhibition. What did the exhibition afford visitors for informal, educationally engaging exhibit experiences?

Aspects are the building blocks, the defining qualities, that form the Framework's Criteria. Aspects provide concrete examples of the kinds of things covered by each Criterion. There are four to eight Aspects for every Criterion. No single exhibition is expected to meet all the Aspects of a Criterion.

Call-outs are notes written during and at the end of an exhibition visit. During the process of using the Framework in an exhibition, a judge writes notes that describe his or her feelings about both details and overall impressions. These are used as evidence for assessing the Aspects. They are primarily for the judge's use but may be shared later in discussions about the exhibition.

Criteria are the standards by which exhibitions are judged. The Framework's Criteria are essential and must be present in an exhibition if visitors are to be afforded excellent learning opportunities.

Excellence is the state of being outstandingly good and of exceptional merit based on particular virtues, in our case those identified in the Framework.

Excellent Judges are museum practitioners who strive for excellence in museum exhibitions, using the Framework as a guide.

Exhibitions are rooms or bounded spaces that contain a group of thematically related exhibit elements. Typically a title identifies the topic or theme. Exhibits are individual components within an exhibition.

The **Framework** is a document and a process to help museum practitioners assess the informal learning opportunities in exhibitions from a visitor-centered perspective, primarily for the purpose of professional development.

Judging is a process of thinking, forming an opinion, deciding on the relative value or worth, and holding something up against standards, guidelines, or criteria.

Ratings are the numbers and rubrics given by judges for each Criterion. There are six levels: 1=Excellent, 2=Very Good, 3=Good, 4=Acceptable, 5=Missed Opportunities, and 6=Counterproductive. Ratings are based on the presence or absence of evidence of the Framework's Aspects seen by the assessor in the exhibition.

Rationales are a judge's reasons for giving a particular rating level to a Criterion. Rationales should use the language of the Aspects to ensure that the scores are internally consistent and to create a growing set of evidence and a shared vocabulary for the group. Rationales and ratings are informed by the judge's Call-outs.

A **visitor-centered perspective** looks at museum exhibitions in terms of what features are present to meet the needs of the end users, the visitors–their expectations, motivations, social agendas, etc.–so that they have a positive learning experience in the exhibition.

164

Bibliography

Allen, S. and J. Gutwill. 2004. "Designing with multiple interactives: Five common pitfalls." *Curator* 47(2): 199-212.

Alt, M. B. and K. M. Shaw. 1984. "Characteristics of ideal museum exhibits." *British Journal of Psychology* 75:25-36.

Ausubel, D. P. 1960. "The use of advance organizers in the learning and retention of meaningful verbal material." *Journal of Educational Research* 51: 267-272.

_____. 1968. *Educational Psychology: A Cognitive View.* New York: Holt, Rinehart, and Winston.

Balling, J. D. and J. H. Falk. 1980. "A perspective on field trips: Environmental effects on learning." *Curator* 23(4): 229-240.

Beaumont, L. 2005. Summative Evaluation of *Wild Reef–Sharks at Shedd.* Unpublished report for the John G. Shedd Aquarium, Chicago.

Bitgood, S. 1990a. "The ABC's of label design." In *Visitor Studies: Theory, Research and Practice,* Vol. 3, eds. S. Bitgood, A. Benefield, and D. Patterson, 115-129. Jacksonville, AL: Center for Social Design.

_____. 1990b. "The role of simulated immersion in exhibition." Technical Report No. 90-20. Jacksonville, AL: Center for Social Design.

_____. 1994. "Designing effective exhibits: Criteria for success, exhibit design approaches and research strategies." *Visitor Behavior* 9(4): 4-15.

Bitgood, S. and A. Benefield. 1995. "Critical appraisal of the Heart Exhibition at the Franklin Institute." *Visitor Behavior* 10(4): 14-16.

Bitgood, S., D. Patterson, and A. Benefield. 1988. "Exhibit design and visitor behavior: Empirical relationships." *Environment and Behavior* 20(4): 474-491.

Bitgood, S., B. Serrell, and D. Thompson. 1994. "The impact of informal education on visitors to museums." In *Informal Science Learning: What the Research Says About Television, Science Museums, and Community-Based Projects,* eds. V. Crane, H. Nicholson, M. Chen, and S. Bitgood, 61-106. Dedham, MA: Research Communications Limited.

Blackmon, C. P., T. K. McMaster, L. C. Roberts, and B. Serrell, eds. 1988. *Open Conversations: Strategies for Professional Development in Museums.* Chicago: Department of Education, Field Museum.

Borun, M. and B. K. Flexer. 1984. "The impact of a class visit to a participatory science museum exhibit and a classroom science lesson." *Journal of Research in Science Teaching* 21(9): 863-873.

Borun, M. and M. Miller. 1980. *What's in a Name?* Philadelphia: The Franklin Institute.

Borun, M., M. B. Chambers, and A. Cleghorn. 1996. "Families are learning in science museums." *Curator* 39(2): 124-138.

Borun, M., M. B. Chambers, J. Dritsas, and J. I. Johnson. 1997. "Enhancing family learning through exhibits." *Curator* 40(4): 279-295.

Borun, M., J. Dritsas, J. I. Johnson, N E. Peter, K. F. Wagner, K. Fadigan, A. Jangaard, E. Stroup, A. Wenger. 1998. *Family Learning in Museums: The PISEC Perspective.* Philadelphia: The Franklin Institute.

Bransford, J. D. 1993. *The Ideal Problem Solver.* New York: W. H. Freeman and Company.

_____. 1979. *Human Cognition, Learning, Understanding, and Remembering.* Belmont, CA: Wadsworth Publishing Company.

Bransford, J. D., R. Sherwood, N. Vye, and J. Rieser. 1986. "Teaching thinking and problem solving: Research foundations." *American Psychologist* 41(10):1078-1089.

Brown, S. P. 1999. "Satisfaction from the visitor perspective." Paper presented at the Visitor Studies Association conference in Chicago.

Chambers, Marlene. 1990. "Beyond 'Aha!': Motivating museum visitors." In *What Research Says about Learning in Science Museums,* Vol. 1, ed. B. Serrell, 10-12. Washington, DC: Association of Science-Technology Centers.

_____. 1999. "Forum: Critiquing exhibition criticism." *Museum News* September/October: 31-37, 65.

_____. 2002. "Intention does count." *NAME Exhibitionist* 21(2): 16-20.

Chambers, M., M. McColly, S. Olsen, J. Terrell, T. C. Thompson, R. Woltman. 1988. "Visitor experience and exhibit context." In *Open Conversations: Strategies for Professional Development in Museums*, eds. C. P. Blackmon, T. K. LaMaster, L. C. Roberts, B. Serrell, 52-54. Chicago: Department of Education, Field Museum.

Crane, V., H. Nicholson, M. Chen, and S. Bitgood, eds. 1994. *Informal Science Learning: What the Research Says About Television, Science Museums, and Community-Based Projects*. Dedham, MA: Research Communications Limited.

Csikszentmihalyi, M. 1990a. "Literacy and intrinsic motivation." *Daedalus* 119(2): 115-140.

_____. 1990b. *Flow: The Psychology of Optimal Experience*. New York: Harper Collins Publishers.

Csikszentmihalyi, M. and K. Hermanson. 1995a. "Intrinsic motivation in museums: What makes visitors want to learn?" *Museum News* 74(3): 34-37, 59-61.

_____. 1995b. "Intrinsic motivation in museums: Why does one want to learn?" In *Public Institutions for Personal Learning: Establishing a Research Agenda*, eds. J. H. Falk and L. D. Dierking, 67-77. Washington, DC: American Association of Museums.

Davidson, B. 1991. *New Dimensions for Traditional Dioramas: Multisensory Additions for Access, Interest and Learning*. Boston: Museum of Science.

Derryberry, M. 1941. "Exhibits." *American Journal of Public Health* 31: 257-263.

Dillenburg, Eugene. 2002. "Sailing into the known." *NAME Exhibitionist* 21(2): 16-20.

Dillenburg, Eugene, L. Friman, and J. Sims. 2001. "Excellence in exhibition." *NAME Exhibitionist* 20(1): 8-13.

Dillenburg, Eugene, Beverly Serrell, Pat Hamilton, Steve Boyd-Smith, Dan Spock, Sue Allen, Robert Garfinkle. 2003. "Listening in: Professionals discuss excellence in exhibition." Panel session at the ASTC annual meeting, St. Paul, MN. Audiocassette.

Dotzour, A., C. Houston, G. Manubay, K. Schulz, and J. C. Smith. 2002. Crossing the Bog of Habits: An evaluation of an exhibit's effectiveness in promoting environmentally responsible behaviors. Master's Thesis, School of Natural Resources and Environment, University of Michigan.

Evans, G. 1995. "Learning and the physical environment." In *Public Institutions for Personal Learning: Establishing a Research Agenda*, eds. J. H. Falk and L. D. Dierking, 119-126. Washington, DC: American Association of Museums.

Falk, J. H. and L. D. Dierking. 1992. *The Museum Experience*. Washington, DC: Whalesback Books.

_____, eds. 1995. *Public Institutions for Personal Learning: Establishing a Research Agenda*. Washington, DC: American Association of Museums.

_____. 2000. "The physical context." In *Learning from Museums: Visitor Experiences and the Making of Meaning*, 53-67. Walnut Creek, CA: AltaMira Press.

Falk, J., W. Martin, and J. Balling. 1978. "The novel field-trip phenomenon: Adjustment to novel settings interferes with task learning." *Journal of Research in Science Teaching* 15(2): 127-134.

Feher, E. and K. Rice. 1985. "Development of scientific concepts through the use of interactive exhibits in museums." *Curator* 28(1):35-46.

Frederiksen, J. R. and B. Y. White. 1997. "Reflective assessment of students' research within an inquiry-based middle school science curriculum." Paper presented at the annual meeting of the American Educational Research Association in Chicago.

_____. (1998) "Video portfolio assessment: Creating a framework for viewing the functions of teaching." *Educational Assessment* 5(4): 225-297.

Frederiksen, John R. and A. Collins. 1996. "Designing an assessment system for the workplace of the future." In *Linking School and Work: Roles for Standards and Assessment*, eds. L. B. Resnick, J. Wirt, and D. Jenkins. San Francisco: Jossey-Bass.

_____. 1989. "A systems approach to educational testing." *Educational Researcher* 18(9): 27-32.

Frederiksen, John R., Mike Sipusic, Miriam Gamoran, and Ed Wolfe. 1992. "Video Portfolio Assessment." Princeton, NJ: Educational Testing Service.

Gagné, R. M. 1985. *The Conditions of Learning*, 4th ed. New York: Holt, Rinehart, and Winston.

Gardner, Howard. 1983. *Frames of Mind: The Theory of Multiple Intelligences*. New York: Basic Books.

Griggs, S. A. 1983. "Orienting visitors within a thematic display." *International Journal of Museum Management and Curatorship* 2:119-134.

_____. 1990. "Perceptions of traditional and new style exhibitions at the Natural History Museum, London." *ILVS Review: A Journal of Visitor Behavior* 1(1): 78-90.

Grunig, J. E. 1980. "Communication of science information to nonscientists." In *Progress in Communicating Sciences,* eds. B. Dervin and M. Voigt, 167-214. Norwood, NJ: Aldev Publishing.

Harvey, M. L. 1995. "The influence of exhibit space design features on visitor attention." Doctoral dissertation, Colorado State University.

Harvey, M. L., M. Marino, and R. Loomis. 1996. "Design features which encourage psychological flow in museum visitors." In *Visitor Studies: Theory, Research and Practice,* Vol. 9, 239-246. Jacksonville, AL: Center for Social Design.

Hayward, D. G. and M. L. Brydon-Miller. 1984. "Spatial and conceptual Aspects of orientation: Visitor experiences at an outdoor history museum." *Journal of Environmental Education* 13(4): 317-332.

Hedge, Alan. 1995. "Human-factor considerations in the design of museums to optimize their impact on learning." In *Public Institutions for Personal Learning: Establishing a Research Agenda,* eds. J. H. Falk and L. D. Dierking, 105-117. Washington, DC: American Association of Museums.

Hein, G. 1998. *Learning in the Museum.* New York: Routledge.

Herrmann, D. and D. Plude. 1995. "Museum memory." In *Public Institutions for Personal Learning: Establishing a Research Agenda,* eds. J. H. Falk and L. D. Dierking, 53-66. Washington, DC: American Association of Museums.

Hilke, D. D., E. C. Hennings, and M. Springuel. 1988. "The impact of interactive computer software on visitors' experiences: A case of study." *ILVS Review: A Journal of Visitor Behavior* 1(1):34-49.

Hirschi, K. D. and C. G. Screven. 1988. "Effects of questions on visitor reading behavior." *ILVS Review: A Journal of Visitor Behavior* 1(1):50-61.

Hood, M. 1993. "Comfort and caring: Two essential environmental factors." *Environment and Behavior* 25(6): 710-724.

Horn, Robert E. 1998. *Visual Language: Global Communication for the 21st Century.* Bainbridge Isle, WA: MacroVU Press.

Institute for Learning Innovation. 2003. *Genetics: Decoding Life*, Supplemental Summative Evaluation. A report for the Museum of Science and Industry, Chicago.

Jarrett, J. E. 1986. "Learning from developmental testing of exhibits." *Curator* 29(4): 295-306.

Jones, J. 2001. "Patronizing, cynical...how did the British Museum get its Cleopatra exhibition so wrong?" *Guardian* (April 14).

Kintsch, W. 1994. "Text comprehension, memory, and learning." *American Psychologist* 49(4): 294-303.

Kool, R. 1988. "Museums and romance: The heart of the subject." In *Open Conversations: Strategies for Professional Development in Museums,* eds. C. P. Blackmon, T. K. McMaster, L. C. Roberts, B. Serrell, p. 44. Chicago: Department of Education, Field Museum.

Koran, J. J., J. S. Foster, and M. L. Koran. 1989. "The relationship among interest, attention and learning in a natural history museum." *Visitor Studies: Theory, Research, and Practice,* Vol. 2, 239-244, eds. S. Bitgood, J. T. Roper, and A. Benefield. Jacksonville, AL: Center for Social Design.

Koran, J. J., M. L. Koran and J. S. Foster. 1988. "Individual differences in learning in informal settings." In *Visitor Studies: Theory, Research and Practice,* eds. S. Bitgood, J. T. Roper, and A. Benefield, 66-70. Jacksonville, AL: Center for Social Design.

Koran, J. J., L. Morrison, L. J. Lehman, M. L. Koran, and L. Gandara. 1984. "Attention and curiosity in museums." *Journal of Research in Science Teaching* 21(4): 357-363.

Korn, Randi & Associates. 1999. A summative evaluation of the *Milky Way Galaxy.* Unpublished report for The Adler Planetarium and Astronomy Museum, Chicago.

Landay, J. and R. G. Bridge. 1982. "Video vs. wall-panel display: An experiment in museum learning." *Curator* 25(1): 41-56.

Leinhardt, Gaea and Karen Knutson. 2004. *Listening in on Museum Conversations.* Walnut Creek, CA: AltaMira Press.

Malone, T. W. 1981. "Toward a theory of intrinsically motivating instruction." *Cognitive Science* 4: 333-69.

Matusov, E. and B. Rogoff. 1995. "Evidence of development from people's participation in communities of learners." In *Public Institutions for Personal Learning: Establishing a Research Agenda*, eds. J. H. Falk and L. D. Dierking, 97-104. Washington, DC: American Association of Museums.

McLean, K. and C. McEver. 2004. *Are We There Yet? Conversations about Best Practices in Science Exhibition Development.* San Francisco: The Exploratorium.

McManus, Paulette. 1986. "Reviewing the reviewers: Towards a critical language for didactic science exhibitions." *The International Journal of Museum Management and Curatorship* 5: 213-226.

_____. 1989. "Oh yes they do: How museum visitors read labels and interact with exhibit texts." *Curator* 32(3): 174-189.

Melton, A. 1935. "Problems of installation in museums of art." AAM Monographs New Series No. 14. (Reprinted by the American Association of Museums, 1988.)

_____. 1972. "Visitor behavior in museums: Some early research in environmental design." *Human Factors* 14(5): 393-403.

Miles, R. S. 1986. "Lessons in human biology: Testing a theory of exhibition design." *International Journal of Museum Management and Curatorship* 5(5): 227-240.

_____. 1988. "Exhibit evaluation in the British Museum (Natural History)," *ILVS Review: A Journal of Visitor Behavior* 1(1): 24-33.

Minnich, Elizabeth. 2003. "Teaching thinking: Moral and political considerations." *Change* September/October, 19-24.

Museum Learning Collaborative's Annotated Literature. www.museumlearning.com/Annotatedlit.html

National Association for Museum Exhibition (NAME). 1994. "The Critical Issue." *NAME Exhibitionist* 13(1).

_____. 1999. "Making meaning in exhibits." *NAME Exhibitionist* 18(2).

_____. 2000. "Critiquing exhibits: Meanings and realities." *NAME Exhibitionist* 19(2).

_____. 2001. "Striving for excellence in exhibitions." *NAME Exhibitionist* 20(1).

_____. 2002. "Critics' choice." *NAME Exhibitionist* 21(2).

National Park Service. 1997. "Interpretive curriculum services and process." www.nps.gov/learn/ (now see Interpretive Development Program IDP page. "Interpretation embraces a discussion of human values, conflicts, ideas, tragedies, achievements, ambiguities, and triumphs.")

Ogbu, J. U. 1995. "The influence of culture on learning and behavior." In *Public Institutions for Personal Learning: Establishing a Research Agenda,* eds. J. H. Falk and L. D. Dierking, 79-95. Washington, DC: American Association of Museums.

Ogden, J., D. Lindburg, and T. Maple. 1993. "The effects of ecologically relevant sounds on zoo visitors." *Curator* 36(2): 147-156.

Patterson, D. and S. Bitgood. 1988. "Some evolving principles of visitor behavior." In *Visitor Studies: Theory, Research and Practice,* eds. S. Bitgood, J. T. Roper, and A. Benefield, 40-50. Jacksonville, AL: Center for Social Design.

Peart, B. 1984. "Impact of exhibit type on knowledge gain, attitudes, and behavior." *Curator* 27(3): 220-227.

Perlow, Leslie. 2003. *When You Say Yes But Mean No: How Silencing Conflict Wrecks Relationships and Companies ... and What You Can Do About It.* New York: Crown Business.

Rabineau, Phyllis. 1994. "An editor's guide to writing criticism." *NAME Exhibitionist* 13(1): 31-32.

Rounds, J. 2002. "Is there a core literature in museology?" *Curator* 44(2): 194-206.

Saunders, C. and E. Perry. 1997 "Summative evaluation of *The Swamp*: A conservation exhibit with a big idea." *Visitor Behavior,* 12(1 & 2): 4-7.

Saunders, C., A. Birjulin, L. Bacon, and T. Gieseke. 1999. "Can an exhibit affect visitor conservation behaviors?" A study conducted at Brookfield Zoo and a poster presented at the annual conference of the Visitor Studies Association in Chicago.

Screven, C. G. 1973. "Public access learning: Experimental studies in a public museum." In *The Control of Human Behavior:* Vol. 3, eds. R. Ulrich, T. Stachnik, and J. Mabry. Glenview, IL: Scott-Foresman.

_____. 1974. *The Measurement and Facilitation of Learning in the Museum Environment: An Experimental Analysis.* Washington, DC: Smithsonian Press.

_____. 1975. "The effectiveness of guidance devices on visitor learning." *Curator* 18(3): 21943.

_____. 1999. *Visitor Studies Bibliography and Abstracts,* 4th edition. Chicago: Screven and Associates.

Selinda Research Associates. 2002. *Underground Adventure:* Summative Evaluation. Unpublished report for Field Museum, Chicago.

Selinda Research Associates. 2003. *Genetics* exhibition: summative evaluation. Unpublished report for Museum of Science and Industry, Chicago.

Semper, Robert J. 1990. "Science museums as environments for learning." *Physics Today,* 43(11): 50-56.

Serrell, Beverly. 1991. *"Learning and learning disabilities: Explorations of the Human Brain* (Museum of Science and Industry, Chicago, a new permanent exhibit opened in spring 1989)." *Journal of Museum Education* 16(2) and 16(3).

_____. 1993. "Awards for exhibits–What are they based on?" *Curator* 36(1): 6-7.

_____. 1994. "Criticism and audience." *NAME Exhibitionist* 13(1): 8-9.

_____. 1998. *Paying Attention: Visitors and Museum Exhibitions.* Washington, DC: American Association of Museums.

_____. 1999. "The 1999 exhibition competition." *Museum News* 78(5): 49-51.

_____. 2001. "A tool for judging excellence in museum exhibitions." *NAME Exhibitionist* 20(1): 16-20.

_____. 2002. "Can't get no satisfaction." *NAME Exhibitionist* 21(2,): 16-20.

Serrell, Beverly, Barbara Becker, and Eugene Dillenburg. 2003. "A framework for assessing exhibitions from a visitor perspective." Panel session at the American Association of Museums annual meeting, Portland, OR. Audiocassette.

Serrell, Beverly, Eugene Dillenburg, Charlie Walters, and Colleen Blair. 2002. "Can we talk? Building a language for judging the visitor experience." Panel session at the American Association of Museums annual meeting, Dallas. Audiocassette.

Shettel, Harris. 1968. "An evaluation of existing Criteria for judging the quality of science exhibits." *Curator* 11(2): 137-153.

_____. 1973. "Exhibits: Art form or educational medium?" *Museum News* 52: 32-41.

_____. 1994. "What can we learn from 'N=1'?" *NAME Exhibitionist* 13(1): 12-13.

_____. 1995. "Should the 51% solution have a caution label?" *Visitor Behavior* 10(3): 10-13.

Silverman, L. 1990. Of us and other "things": The content and functions of talk by adult visitor pairs in an art and a history museum. Doctoral dissertation, University of Pennsylvania.

Spillman, Jane. 1993. "An answer to 'What are the curators committee awards for?'" *Curator* 36(2): 86-88.

Wolf, R. 1992. "The missing link: The role of orientation in enriching the museum experience." In *Patterns in Practice: Selections from the Journal of Museum Education*, ed. K. Nichols, 134-143. Washington, DC: Museum Education Roundtable, Inc.

Zueck, V. M. 1988. "Conceptual organizers and goal setting in the Milwaukee Public Museum." Doctoral dissertation, University of Wisconsin-Milwaukee.

Photo Credits

Page 8: Project advisors, by Eugene Dillenburg. Page 11: Beverly in Mikva's robe, by author. Page 13: Videotaping at The Cliff Dwellers, by author. Page 22: Marisa in *Play It Safe*, Chicago Children's Museum, by author. Page 26: *Underground Adventure*, by author, with permission of Field Museum. Page 35: At Adler Planetarium & Astronomy Museum, *Milky Way Galaxy*, by author. Page 47: First meeting; by author. Pages 50 and 51: Left to right, exterior of *The Swamp* at Brookfield Zoo, by Hannah Jennings; Chicago Historical Society exterior, by author; entry to *Amazon Rising* at Shedd Aquarium, by Eugene Dillenburg; entry to *Play It Safe*, Chicago Children's Museum; and sculpture in front of Adler Planetarium, by author. Pages 53 and 54: In *The Swamp*, by author, with permission of Brookfield Zoo. Page 65: Ben in *Inventing Lab* at Chicago Children's Museum, by author. Page 66: *Underground Adventure*, by author, with permission of Field Museum. Cover and Page 68: Kimberly at Adler Planetarium, by author. Page 70: Dan in *Teen Chicago*, reproduced with permission of Chicago Historical Society. Page 75: *Otters and Oil* at Shedd Aquarium, by Eugene Dillenburg. Page 87: In *Statue of an Emperor*, reproduced with permission of The J. Paul Getty Museum, Los Angeles, California. Page 106: Entry to *Amazon Rising* at Shedd Aquarium, by Eugene Dillenburg. Page 108: Peter and Josie in *The Swamp*, by author, with permission of Brookfield Zoo. Page 111: Entry to *The Swamp*, by author, with permission of Brookfield Zoo. Page 121: Courtesy of John R. Frederikson. Page 134: *Wild Reef*, by author, with permission of Shedd Aquarium. Page 138: Big bug in *Underground Adventure*, by author, with permission of Field Museum. Page 146: Beverly at *Risk* at Fort Worth Museum of History and Science, by Eugene Dillenburg. Page 153: Tenth meeting, by author. Page 157: In *The Swamp*, by author, with permission of Brookfield Zoo. Page 160: In *Genetics: Decoding Life*, by author, with permission of Museum of Science and Industry. Pages 178 and 180: By author, at The Cliff Dwellers.

Who Were the Excellent Judges, Anyway?

The Chicago Excellent Judges were a combination of museum professionals who worked for local institutions and as consultants. Almost all of the consultants at some time had also been on staff at one or more of these museums: Adler Planetarium and Astronomy Museum; The Art Institute of Chicago; Brookfield Zoo; Chicago Children's Museum; Field Museum; Museum of Science and Industry; The Oriental Institute; Peggy Notebaert Nature Museum; John G. Shedd Aquarium. Names and job titles are listed below without affiliations because the individuals were representing themselves, not their institutions or companies.

Participants in Fall 2000 pilot program

Clifford Abrams, exhibit designer
Roy Alexander, exhibit designer
Barbara Becker, exhibit developer
Tsivia Cohen, museum educator
Eugene Dillenburg, exhibit developer
Nancy Goodman, exhibit developer
Dianne Hanau-Strain, exhibit designer
Mark Hayward, exhibit developer
Virginia Heidenreich-Barber, exhibit developer
Hannah Jennings, exhibit designer
Kris Nesbitt, exhibit developer
Deborah Perry, exhibit evaluator
Therese Quinn, museum educator
Beverly Serrell, museum consultant

When we got the grant from National Science Foundation to continue our investigations with more focus and a research question, many of the EJs from the first round were joined by some new faces.

Participants in Chicago for the NSF 2002-2003 program

Barbara Becker, exhibit developer
Barbara Ceiga, exhibit developer
Diane Gutenkauf, exhibit developer
Dianne Hanau-Strain, exhibit designer
Hannah Jennings, exhibit designer
Jennifer Johnston, exhibit developer
Shauna E. Keane-Timberlake, evaluator
Frank Madsen, exhibit designer
Beverly Serrell, museum consultant

Participants Gutenkauf, Hanau-Strain, and Ceiga.

Advisors and participants Becker, Ansbacher, Ratcliff, Serrell, Weiss, Allen, and Dillenburg are pictured on page 8.

The advisors were selected because they represented a range of exhibit expertise and respected institutions.

NSF 2002-2003 National Advisors

Sue Allen and Joshua Gutwill,
    The Exploratorium, San Francisco
Ted Ansbacher,
    museum consultant, White Plains, N.Y.
Eugene Dillenburg,
    Science Museum of Minnesota, St. Paul
Rachel Hellenga,
    The Tech Museum, San Jose, Calif.
Stephanie Ratcliff,
    Maryland Science Center, Baltimore
Martin Weiss,
    New York Hall of Science, Queens, N.Y.

West Coast participants who tried out an earlier version of the Framework at the Getty in August 2003:

Marni Gittleman, museum educator
Lynn LaBate, curator
Ann Marshall, designer
Viviane Meerbergen, museum educator
Mary Beth Trautwein, designer

Fresh Chicago participants recruited to test out the semifinal version in September 2003:

Dave Becker, educator
Tamara Biggs, exhibit developer
Joy Bivens, curator
Eliza Duenow, museum educator
Bruce Styler, designer
Jackie Terrassa, museum educator
Bennie Welch, designer

In St. Paul, Minn., EJs met for the Association of Science-Technology Centers conference in 2003 and presented a panel discussion about the *Mississippi River Gallery* at the Science Museum of Minnesota:

Sue Allen, visitor studies researcher
Robert Garfinkle, exhibit developer
Pat Hamilton, exhibit developer
Steve Boyd Smith, Web producer and
 exhibit developer
Dan Spock, designer and exhibit developer

In the video on the CD, the Excellent Judges were:

Barbara Becker, exhibit developer
Tamara Biggs, exhibit developer
Joy Bivens, curator
Hannah Jennings, exhibit designer
Frank Madsen, exhibit designer
Beverly Serrell, museum consultant

Stars of the Excellent Judges video, left to right: Becker, Jennings, Biggs, Serrell, Madsen, Bivens.

About the Chapter Contributors

SUE ALLEN is the director of visitor research and evaluation at the Exploratorium in San Francisco.

BARBARA BECKER is an independent museum professional living in Chicago, who does exhibit planning, development and evaluation. Becker was formerly on staff at Field Museum and Shedd Aquarium.

BEN DICKOW is the manager of program development and training at the California Science Center. Dickow was formerly on staff at the Museum of Science and Industry, Chicago.

EUGENE DILLENBURG is an exhibit developer and haiku master at The Science Museum of Minnesota, St. Paul. Dillenburg was formerly on staff at Field Museum and Shedd Aquarium.

HANNAH JENNINGS is an independent designer and developer in Oak Park, Ill., and a former President of the Society for Environmental Graphic Design. Jennings was formerly on staff as head of the design department at Brookfield Zoo.

LYNN LABATE is an independent curator who specializes in Latin American art and culture. Previously LaBate was on staff at the Fullerton Museum Center in Orange County, Calif., and was an education specialist at the J. Paul Getty Museum.

MARY BETH TRAUTWEIN is an independent designer and developer in Los Angeles, and was formerly an exhibition designer at the J. Paul Getty Museum.

Index

About the Author

Beverly Serrell has served the museum community since 1979 as a consultant, workshop leader, speaker, and author on topics related to the conception, development, and evaluation of exhibitions of all kinds and sizes. Before that, she was curator of education at Shedd Aquarium for eight years. She likes rock and roll, spicy food, and fireworks. For more information, please visit www.serrellassociates.org.